A Century of American Toys & Games

The Story of Pressman Toy

Jim Pressman & Donna Pressman

With Alan Axelrod

A Century of American Toys & Games

The Story of Pressman Toy

Pressman Toy

Abbeville Press Publishers
New York London

Contents

Hop Ching Chinese Checkers, 1949.

Chapter 1
Beginnings
1896–1938

How does a privately owned family-run company, a toy company founded in 1922, last one hundred years? And how does it not only survive, but flourish as the maker and marketer of many of the bestselling and most iconic board games in the world?

This is the story of Pressman Toy Corporation, starting with its humble beginnings in the days when a twenty-seven-year-old Jack Pressman built his earliest business on such idiosyncratic products as the *Zellopiano* and on emerging fads like *Chinese Checkers*. This is the story of a genuine family business, which was itself transformed when the founder met and married Lynn Rambach, who was instrumental in running the company while Jack Pressman was still in his prime and, even more, during the period of ill health that ended in his untimely death in 1959. At that point, Lynn became one of America's pioneer female CEOs, a rarity in all American industries and nearly unheard of in the world of toys.

From Lynn, the torch was passed to their youngest child, Jim Pressman, under whose leadership, beginning in 1977, the company enjoyed its greatest successes.

LEFT
The Pressman store in Harlem sold novelties, sporting goods, and toys. This 1916 photo shows (*from left to right*) Abraham "Pop" Pressman, employee Nathan Leibowitz, and Abe's son Jack Pressman, twenty years old at the time.

RIGHT
Bill Pressman, Jack's younger brother, sent this letter to Jim Pressman in 1995, along with the 1916 photograph.

A Little Shop in Harlem

Before there was a Pressman Toy Company, there was a shop in New York's Harlem, a variety store Jack Pressman's father, Abraham, opened some time after he took flight from the deadly anti-Semitic pogroms that frequently ravaged the "Pale," a region straddling czarist Russia and Poland within which Jewish settlement was forcibly confined.

As it did for generations of immigrants, America beckoned Abe Pressman as a place of tolerance, liberty, and opportunity. In steerage, on the transatlantic crossing, he met the young woman who would become his bride, Fanny Fingerhut.

In New York, Abe and Fanny raised three boys — George the eldest, Bill the youngest, and Jack, the middle brother. By the time of Jack's birth, in 1896, the family was living on Manhattan's Upper East Side, in the Yorkville neighborhood, not very far from the variety store in Harlem. It sold candy and "novelties," a catchall category that included sporting goods and playthings, among other small merchandise. Brother George eventually studied dentistry, but, in 1916, Jack went to work in his father's store. There, he became acquainted with toy jobbers such as Nathan Leibowitz, and while his father taught him how to sell toys from behind a store counter, Nathan and others schooled him in the business of making and marketing toys.

Soon, Jack was hooked on the toy business and doubtless would have immediately launched his own company had it not been for America's entry into World War I. Like some four million other American lads, Jack Pressman suddenly found himself in the uniform of a doughboy, and although he never shipped out to France, he served in the U.S. Army from April 5, 1918, to May 28, 1919.

TOP
Jack Pressman's Selective Service registration card.

BOTTOM
Jack Pressman's U.S. Army discharge form from 1919.

LEFT
Jack with brother Bill.

TOP RIGHT
The first ad from Jack Pressman & Co., December 1923. The ad on the lower half of the page is for North American Toy Co., in which Jack had become a partner one year earlier. They were now one company.

BOTTOM RIGHT
Playthings ad from January 1924.

OPPOSITE
An early Pressman *Zellophone* toy, complete with its colorful box.

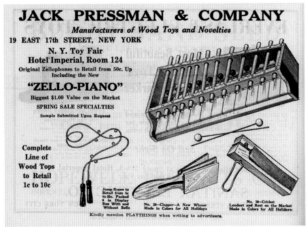

The Company Is Born

Following his discharge, Jack became a salesman of metal toys for M. Gropper & Sons, a Brooklyn-based maker of a wide variety of playthings. Then, in 1922, Jack joined the North American Toy Company as a partner. The company was a toy jobber, a modest wholesaler, but it now began, on a small scale, manufacturing its own toys, including lead soldiers and *Zellophones*, a toy-size version of the traditional xylophone. After Jack joined the company, North American became J. Pressman & Company.

The new toymaker received its first notice in the toy industry press when the company showed its wares at the New York Toy Fair in January 1924: "Jack Pressman & Co is showing a very attractive line of wooden peg toys, jump ropes and noise makers to retail at very attractive prices." Jack told the reporter that the company was experiencing "excellent demand for the 'Zellopiano,'" which, the article elaborated, "offers wonderful value at $1.00 retail." A toy-size hybrid of a xylophone and piano, the *Zellopiano* had piano-style keys, which, when played, caused "hammers to strike the brass tubes tuned to the scale."

Judging from this early 1924 article, J. Pressman & Co. was already operating with the merchandise-mix strategy that would define the enterprise throughout its long life. The foundation of its offerings consisted of traditional, simple toys — peg toys, jump ropes, noise makers — to which were added a few new and original items, such as the *Zellopiano*.

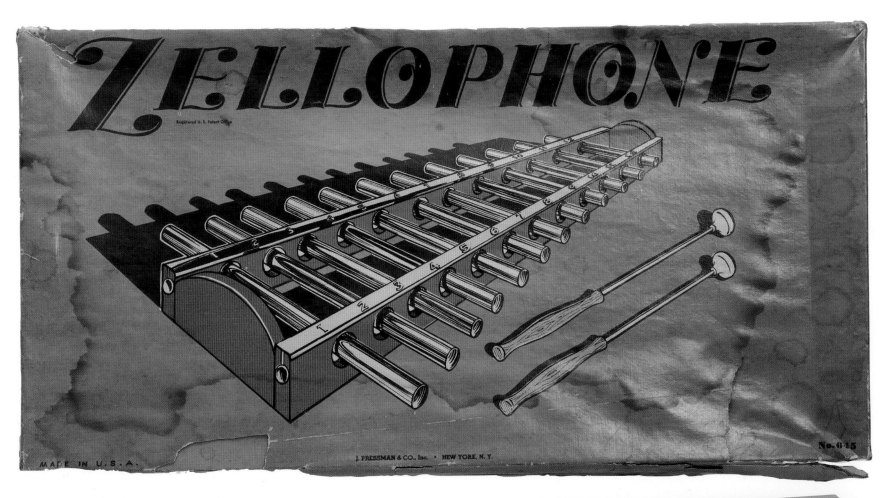

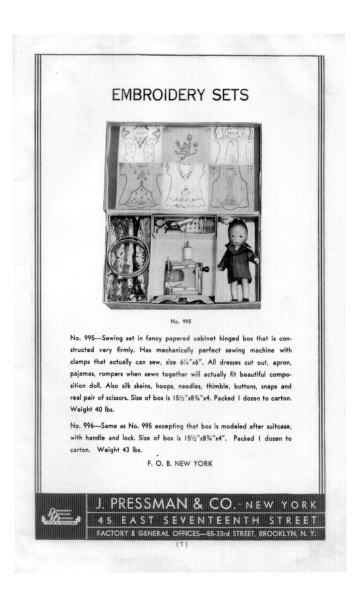

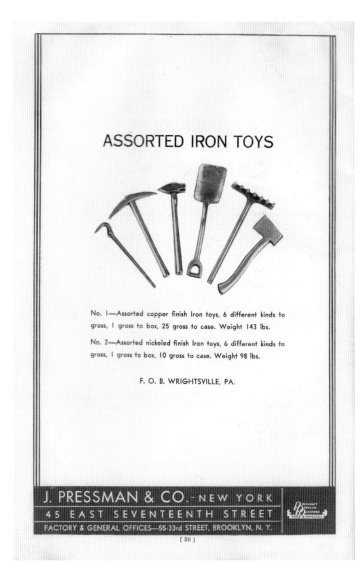

This embroidery set is an example of Pressman's diverse early line. It was offered in a variety of sizes and prices.

Jacks were a Pressman staple for many years. They were offered in copper, nickel plate, or painted in red, white, and blue. The jack stones could be bought in a set, complete with ball and bag, or separately.

In a world before the advent of plastic, toys were made using wood, paper, and metal. The assortment of Pressman iron toys included picks, hammers, rakes, and axes. Hard to believe that these were sold to children as playthings!

THIS PAGE AND OPPOSITE
Selections from Pressman's 1932 catalog.

Birth of an Industry

A history of the American toy industry published in 1924 provides a snapshot of the field into which J. Pressman & Co. was making its entrance. Many commentators saw "the recent World War" as providing the impetus to launch a U.S. domestic toy industry. They pointed out that, prior to 1914, the year World War I began in Europe, most American children played with toys that were imported from Europe, especially Germany, or were homemade. To be sure, the wartime interruption of German exports did create an opportunity for the domestic manufacture of American toys.

Thanks to the rise of the middle class, the shift away from a primarily agrarian culture, and the rise of leisure time among children, toys became viable for a broad audience that had not previously existed. A testament to this growth was the creation of the Toy Manufacturers of America. A group of the leading companies came together in 1916 to create this organization and secured their first office in the Flatiron Building in Manhattan.

The Tariff Act of 1922, which levied duties of up to 70 percent on toys being imported from Japan and Germany, also fueled the young industry's growth.

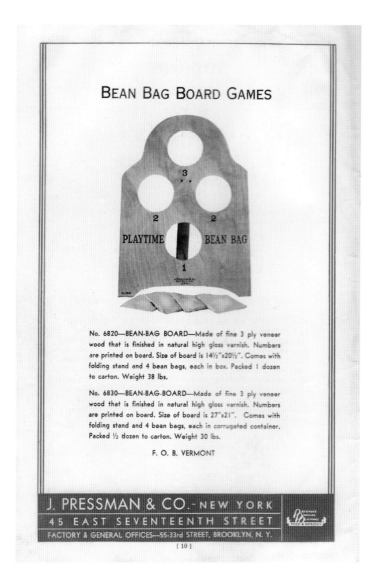

Bean Bag and *Bollo Ball* were early hits for Pressman.
Bolo Ball later became *Skill Ball.*

JACK PRESSMAN & CO.
Nathan Leibowitz and Jack Pressman

The Early Pressman Line

This February 1928 photograph is the earliest image of the Pressman Toy Showroom as it appeared at the Toy Fair that year. Nathan Leibowitz is on the left, Jack on the right, and there are lots of *Zellopianos*!

The 1920s brought a general postwar boom in the manufacture and sales of consumer goods, especially toys, as a Progressive "culture of the child" developed, in which children became a major commercial market. Thus, the early 1920s were an opportune time to start a toy company, and, in 1925, Jack took on Max Eibetz as a partner. While Eibetz ran the company's Brooklyn factory at 346 Carroll Street, Jack took care of sales in Manhattan, from an office at 46 East 47th Street. He also tended to his younger brother, Bill, after their mother, Fanny, suffered an emotional breakdown and was taken to a sanitarium in the Catskills. Jack went on to finance Bill's college education – the youngest Pressman having chosen to attend a campus as far

away as he could imagine, the University of Georgia, in the town of Athens. After graduation, Bill returned to the family fold and was hired as sales manager for the company.

With the Carroll Street factory in operation, the February 1926 edition of the industry magazine *Playthings* featured an ad for new Pressman toys ready for spring delivery. These included the familiar *Zellophone* toy xylophone, which was offered in a range of prices, from twenty-five cents to five dollars. New items were featured, including embroidery and sewing sets and an "enameled" game of ten-pins, as well as what Pressman called "some of our fast selling staples." Among these were tops (and top cords), checkers,

15

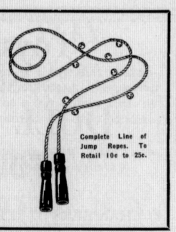
TOP LEFT
Ad from February 1926.

TOP RIGHT
This January 1928 *Playthings* ad features "NEW and Staple Profit-Makers."

BOTTOM
Ad from July 1927.

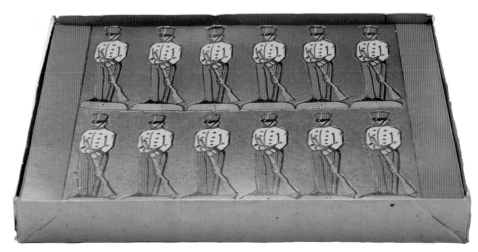

LEFT
This *Playtime Bubble Outfit* from 1932 included two enameled pipes, two cakes of soap, one glass bowl, and, for good measure, one "rubberized" apron.

RIGHT
Soldiers was an early J. Pressman cardboard toy.

jump ropes, noise makers, "liquid pistols" (squirt guns), "furnished fish lines," soldier sets, bead toys, and table croquet.

In January 1928, a Pressman ad once again featured the "staples" but added such new items as a *Complete New Line of Wood Spinning Tops* (ranging from a penny to a dime), a *Playtime Bubble Outfit*, kindergarten scissors, enameled bead dolls, jacks, cast-iron

hatchets, cast-iron hammers, chime toys, pull chime toys, and a ring-toss game.

Playthings reported: the 1928 Toy Fair "room of Jack Pressman & Co.... presented a busy scene... [offering] a large line for the approval of buyers. Among the new things... were noted the 'On Parade' soldier tenpins, 'Bollo-Ball' rolling game, 'Jungle Hunt' bird shooting game, and a snappy line of Juvenile golf outfits."

Chinese Checkers, which J. Pressman sometimes branded as *Hop Ching Checkers*, put the company on the map as the game became an American craze.

TOP ROW
Chinese Checkers games from 1945.

BOTTOM
Hop Ching Checkers, 1949.

Birth of an Icon:
Chinese Checkers

Yet to hit industry news publications was an event that proved to be a major chapter in the Pressman story. During a trip to the American West, Jack Pressman encountered *Chinese Checkers*, a game virtually unknown to the toy industry at the time. But the game has a long genealogy. Its origins are to be found in a game invented and sold in Germany in 1892: *Stern-Halma*. The *Halma* part of the name refers to an older American game, invented in 1883 or 1884 by Dr. George Howard Monks, a thoracic surgeon at Harvard Medical School. In its turn, Monks's American *Halma*

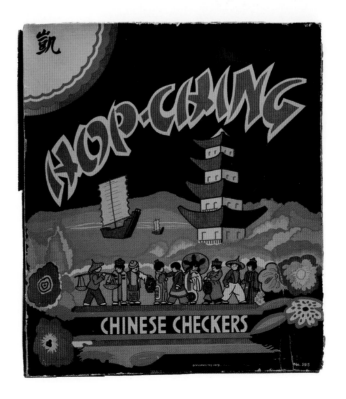

was inspired by *Hoppity*, an English game that apparently first appeared in 1854. As for the *Stern* part of the 1892 German game, *Stern* is the German word for "star" and refers to the star shape of the German board, in contrast to the square board of *Halma*.

In 1935, Jack was so impressed with the possibilities of *Chinese Checkers* that he either acquired or copied the game and put it into immediate production to the exclusion of all other items. His decision triggered a craze for the game that swept the country. Either through incredible prescience or very good luck, Jack had just invested in a toy marble company, which

ensured that J. Pressman & Co. would have a virtually limitless supply of marbles to feed the burgeoning demand for this indispensable *Chinese Checkers* accessory.

The company first brought out *Chinese Checkers* as *Hop Ching Checkers* but soon renamed it *Chinese Checkers* – although the *Hop Ching* version continued to be marketed in parallel for a time. While *Hop Ching* was a fabricated Chinese name and *Chinese Checkers* has no Asian history whatsoever, Jack played off a then-current American vogue for all things "Oriental" and branded the game accordingly.

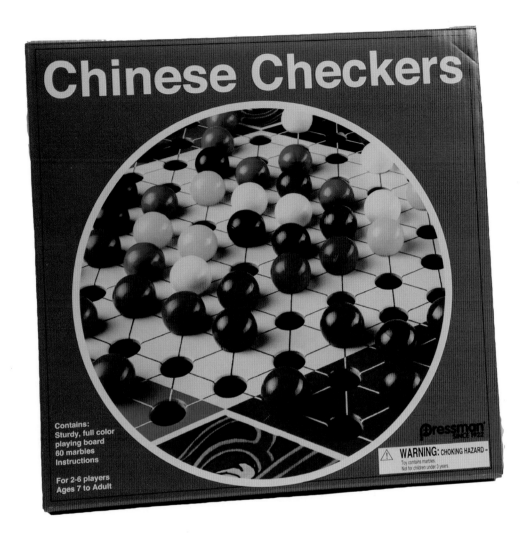

A 1938 article from *Playthings* commented on the American "boom in Chinese Checker games" and noted that between late 1935 and 1938, "fifteen million Chinese Checker games had been sold, utilizing about a billion marbles." Pressman was not the only toymaker producing the game. Indeed (*Playthings* noted), the Burland Printing Company "had produced five million Chinese Checker boards for various manufacturers . . . [which], if piled one on top of another, would reach several times the height of the Empire State Building." Another manufacturer told *Playthings* "that if all the marbles he had used in his games were placed one foot apart at the Equator, they would form a belt entirely around the earth."

But while Pressman was not alone in selling *Chinese Checkers*, the company had a first-mover advantage, which it exploited to the hilt. It not only rode the crest of the initial *Chinese Checkers* sensation but also stuck with the game, becoming the premier brand identified with it as the game transitioned from a fad to one of the staples of American board games. Thus, *Chinese Checkers* emerged as Pressman's first truly "iconic" toy. It would be the first of many.

Pressman's *Chinese Checkers* today.

Playtime Fisherman Outfit, 1930s.

Chapter 2
Pressman's Popular Playthings Face the Great Depression

1932–1938

The 1930s were marked by the Great Depression, an economic cataclysm that posed a daunting challenge not merely to business but to the survival of the nation. Families, many struggling to put food on the table, faced painful spending decisions day by day. Fortunately for American toymakers, the Toy Manufacturers of America succeeded in establishing toys as an "essential" industry. As Christopher Byrne noted in his *Profile of the United States Toy Industry* (first ed., 2013), this designation meant "that the importance of toys and play in the lives of children should accord the industry special status."

The government agreed. More important, so did even financially pinched parents, who did their best to prioritize toys on their shopping lists. The 1930s was thus a decade of growth for Pressman, which, in 1934, moved its Manhattan headquarters seven blocks uptown from 45 East 17th Street to 1107 Broadway. It was now in the heart of the Toy District.

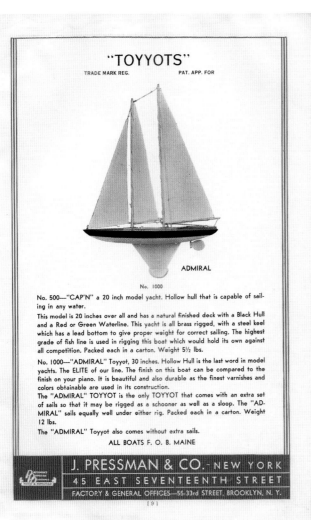

LEFT AND CENTER
Toyyots were "Just a Few of Our Specialties": a page from the 1932 catalog and an ad in *Playthings* from the same year.

TOP RIGHT
The J. Pressman & Co. ad in the March 1935 *Playthings* highlighted the company's move to 1107 Broadway, New York. Gone were Jack's days of running a "showroom" out of a hotel room. J. Pressman & Co. had entered the big leagues.

BOTTOM RIGHT
April 1936 full-page ad from *Playthings*.

Miniature Golf Goes Big

J. Pressman & Co. was determined to partake in the industry's surprisingly strong position by ensuring a high public profile for its newest offerings. As we saw in chapter 1, Jack Pressman "discovered" *Chinese Checkers* during a trip to the American West. It was, in fact, a game with a history going back to the nineteenth century, but it remained all but unknown to American toymakers until Pressman marketed it into a pop culture phenomenon. Jack created a national fad—with legs. It became an enduring classic in the 1930s and beyond.

A look back at a Pressman catalog from 1932 reveals a mix of novel toys with such staples as jump ropes, crayons, jacks, and bingo. That catalog also lists some throwbacks to the sporting goods stocked in Abraham Pressman's original Harlem store. There are "finished" fishing lines, complete with reel, forty-foot cable line, sinker, and hook. There are hockey sticks. And there are golf tees "made of Vermont finest white wood, finished in waterproof bright lacquered colors."

Golf tees are one thing, but the 1932 catalog also offered a whole array of golf paraphernalia scaled down in size and price for children. This included golf bag sets with various combinations of drivers, putters, mashies, and wood balls. Clubs ranged from 28 inches to 32 inches in length, a modest miniaturization of the typical 45.5-inch-long adult driver.

Golf was big in 1930s America, the decade seeing the creation of the tremendously popular Masters Tournament in 1934. Pressman was already producing numerous toys that emulated the adult world of housework, vocations, and professions, and "juvenile" golf sets could be classified as merely the latest addition to such items.

But they were also a response to the new pop culture golf sensation that was sweeping Depression

J. Pressman *Bingo* sets of the 1930s.

24

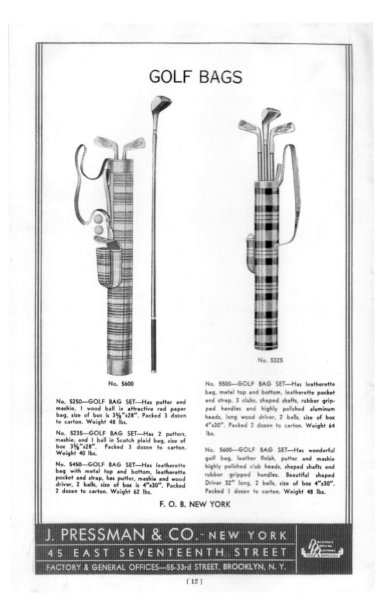

LEFT
Children's golf bag sets from the 1932 catalog.

RIGHT
Miniature golf, 1930s-style: Mary Pickford and Douglas Fairbanks at the opening of Wilshire Links, Beverly Hills, California.

Era America: "miniature" golf, which became even bigger than the full-size sport that spawned it. Miniature golf started as yet another novelty of the Roaring Twenties, but by the early 1930s it exploded into a craze. The year 1930 saw more than forty thousand miniature golf courses burst into being across the country, places with such names as Lilliput Links, Rinky Dink Golf, Tom Thumb Golf, and, more primly, Garden Golf and Baby Golf. Some courses were located outdoors, but many were set up indoors, as free attractions in department stores and restaurants.

"Al Capone Gets a Grip on Toy Golf"

J. Pressman & Co. was hardly the only organization looking to cash in on the miniature golf craze. In "Al Capone Gets a Grip on Toy Golf," Ray Doyle, reporter for the *New York Daily Mirror*, wrote that two of Capone's "torpedoes" told him on October 1, 1930, that "Al . . . has gone into the little golf game in a big way." His organization was "purchasing large blocks of stock in miniature golf construction companies." As one of Al's minions remarked, "It is more profitable than rum running [and will] keep us away from all police and Grand Jury investigations, which are a nuisance to us and waste of time to all concerned."

"Al has gone nut[s] about this miniature golf," Capone's torpedo also told Doyle, and "is fast becoming a star." But of course Scarface was already a star in the firmament of American pop culture. And so it is no accident that the same 1932 Pressman catalog with all the golf paraphernalia also featured *Big Shot Cap Pistols* – the one illustrated looking a lot more like a gangster's .38 than a cowboy's .44 – and *Junior Police Outfits*. These included such items as handcuffs, a badge, a whistle, a billy club, and a hat with a police shield.

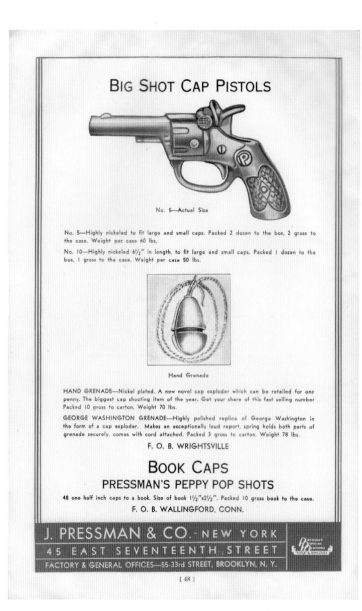

LEFT
In 1932, *Pressman's Peppy Pop Shots* were cap toys ranging from guns to hand grenades.

RIGHT
All you needed to play cop in 1932 – including a "highly polished police club."

J. PRESSMAN & CO., Inc. • NEW YORK, N. Y.

"G-MAN" DETECTIVE SETS

(Continued)

No. 126—"DICK TRACY" DETECTIVE AND FIN-
GERPRINT OUTFIT — A perfect complete set
with all equipment. 80 power Microscope, fingerprint ink, fingerprint powder, glass, roller, magnifying glass, badge and instruction book with
permanent fingerprint record. All in fancy box,
size 13¾″ x 11¾″.

Packed 1 doz. to carton.   Weight 30 lbs.

Price — $144.00 per Gross

F. O. B. New York

[16]

Gangster culture was as much a part of the fabric of life in the 1930s as miniature golf. Not that the year 1932 was auspicious for Al Capone. Throughout the 1920s, he had evaded prosecution. The local cops, of the kind represented in Pressman's 1932 *Junior Police Outfits*, were always one long step behind him, and it took the combined efforts of the FBI and the IRS to finally nail the gangster – on income tax evasion.

The FBI's involvement in bringing Capone to justice put that agency squarely in the spotlight, and the 1937 Pressman catalog replaced the *Junior Police Outfits*, modeled on local law enforcement, with FBI *G-Man Detective Sets*. These added fingerprint ink pads, fingerprint record sheets, "detective powder" (fingerprint dusting powder), and a brush to the handcuffs and badge included in the earlier sets. In a somewhat incongruous move, Pressman also issued its junior G-Men a policeman's whistle.

Dick Tracy in the Funny Papers

In 1938, Pressman turned from the FBI to the funny papers for its model of law enforcement. Dick Tracy debuted in the Sunday comics section of the *Detroit Mirror* on October 4, 1931. As created by Chester Gould, Tracy was a police detective based on the character of real-life G-Man Eliot Ness.

In 1934, the *Dick Tracy* comic strip spawned a radio serial that ran until 1948. The Sunday comic strip was also incarnated in comic books beginning in 1936.

Dick Tracy toy tie-ins began to appear in 1934, and Pressman innovated on its own *G-Man Detective Sets* with a *Dick Tracy Detective and Fingerprint Outfit*, which appeared in 1938. This one represented a considerable advance beyond the generic G-Man set of the preceding year. The catalog described it as a "perfect complete set with all equipment," which was a remarkably accurate representation. Included were an "80 power Microscope, fingerprint ink, fingerprint powder, glass, roller, magnifying glass, badge and instruction book with permanent fingerprint record." The box top featured elaborate Dick Tracy comic-book graphics.

OPPOSITE
The "Dick Tracy" Detective Set and Fingerprint Outfit in the 1937 catalog included an eighty-power microscope

LEFT
The 1932 catalog cover featured the wide range of J. Pressman toys.

CENTER
Cover of J. Pressman's 1937 catalog.

RIGHT
Cover from the 1938 catalog.

Magic sets were top entertainment in the thirties. The 1932 catalog noted of this one: "made not for a magician but for a young boy or girl."

RIGHT
Laundry sets were popular in the thirties. This one from the 1937 catalog featured a sad iron and eight clothespins.

J. PRESSMAN & CO., Inc. • NEW YORK, N. Y.

LAUNDRY SETS

No. 7350—LITTLE MOTHER'S LAUNDRY SET—A practical and useful set for the little helper. Contains wood ironing board, 15" x 4½", Sad iron and 8 clothes pins. All in attractive, lithographed labeled set-up box, size 18" x 5¾" x 1½".

Packed 4 doz. to carton.   Weight 42 lbs.

Price — $36.00 per Gross

F. O. B. New York

[22]

A Dash of Magic and a Pinch of Innocence

Even as many Pressman toys reflected and emulated the adult world, others evoked a realm of fantasy. Such items as *Little Mother's Laundry Set* (containing a wood ironing board, an old-fashioned sad iron, and eight clothespins) and two *Luncheon Sets* (with table-cloths and napkins intended to be embroidered using the silk skeins, needle, hoop, and thimble provided) were defined by the housewife's world. But three different *Magic Shows* and one "larger and more thrilling" *Magic Set* invited children to create their own fantasy space. The three "shows" contained eight, nine, and fourteen tricks, while the larger "set" had "numerous mystifying tricks." Adults and children alike have an urge to transcend mundane reality, and the drab hardships of the Depression era made magicians and magic acts highly popular entertainment in the 1930s.

Featured side by side with the *Magic Show* in the 1932 catalog was the *Fisherman Outfit*. It was "a new and novel fishing game, [which included] 4 fast colored

lacquered wooden fish, size 3″ × 1¼″, which float in water." The set contained a fishing rod and was advertised as a "real game of skill." Action games like the *Fisherman Outfit* would prove an enduring feature of the Pressman line, but, even more significantly, toys and games of this kind kept the company's brand firmly rooted in serving and celebrating the essence of play. For all the company's continually evolving con-nection with popular culture, including the likes of gangsters and G-Men, the demand for toys like the *Fisherman Outfit* never flagged. In fact, fishing games proved so enduringly popular that Pressman makes and markets them to this day. It has never stopped, and the company today sells a million updated battery-operated fishing games annually.

Fishing games were a hit in the 1930s, evolving through the decades into a long-lived favorite today.

One example, from 1938, of the many tiddlywinks games Pressman produced over the years.

Chapter 3
In Action, in the News, and on the Silver Screen

1937–1939

By the 1930s, table tennis, like miniature golf, was sweeping the nation. Anybody with the space and a modicum of spare money could go out and buy a purpose-built table tennis table, but all the Pressman set required was any flat rectangular table. The game could be set up for play and then cleared away just in time for lunch or dinner.

The 1937 catalog is a snapshot of J. Pressman & Co. at the early height of its media, current events, and pop-culture savvy. As always, the company maintained its strong brand identity as a maker of traditional "basic" or "essential" playthings. They were the old standbys familiar not just to kids but, equally important, to their parents, who had a sentimental attachment to the toys, having themselves played with them.

Pressman cultivated a kind of loyalty to these basic playthings. True, there was nothing original or novel about them, but the company wanted to be identified as making their very best versions. When, for example, Pressman offered tiddlywinks (or "Tiddledy Winks," as the company spelled it), it advertised the outfit's uniquely high quality: "A new wink game in a larger and more attractive box than ever before. Has a 3-color varnished platform with cup and 3 sets of colored winks."

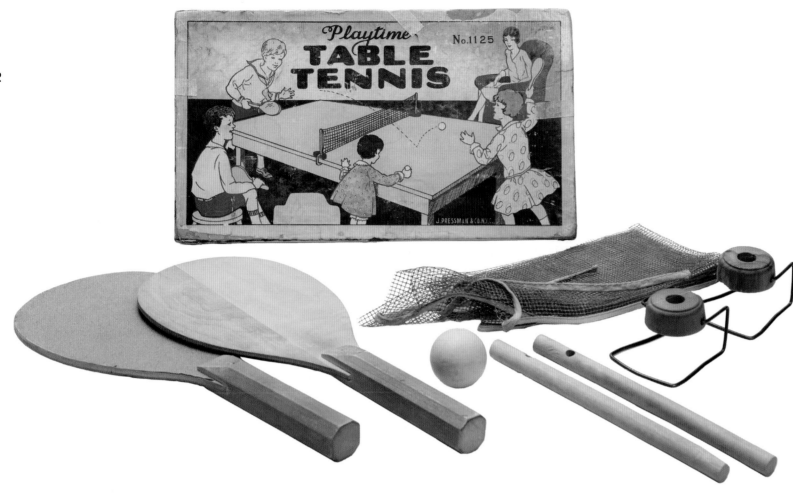

Table tennis exploded in the thirties, and Jack Pressman produced a variety of sets, such as this one from 1937.

In selling toys, Pressman frequently nodded to the cultural connection but first and foremost emphasized the fun. Through all the years, the company counterpointed high-quality versions of bread-and-butter popular traditional toys and games with breakout items and innovations. Increasingly, these featured items were tied to headline-making news, media personalities and sensations, popular entertainment, or some combination of the three. Reflections of the times, the toys sometimes had disturbing implications. The child's game of cops and robbers became, more sinisterly, G-Men versus gangsters. Yet, gritty as some of the reality was, it almost invariably proved translatable into playthings.

Putting the Action in Games

The *Fisherman Outfit*, mentioned in chapter 2, was what we today call an "action game." In contrast to card games and board games, action games challenge and develop physical dexterity. The 1932 Pressman catalog featured *Bean Bag Board Games*, in which players competed in tossing bean bags through holes in an upright board (the harder targets awarded more points), and several versions of *Bollo Board*, in which players rolled balls onto an inclined board with beveled holes worth various points, depending on difficulty.

The Dawn of Licensing

Through the years, Pressman was an innovator and a leader in licensing. Jack was an astute and clear-minded businessman, who knew what he liked and who he liked. He was also a great teacher and innovator, being among the very first business leaders to sign up entertainment licenses.

In 1937, *Fortune* magazine published a popularity poll of comic strips. *Dick Tracy* featured high in the poll, as did *Popeye*, *Blondie*, *Moon Mullins*, *Li'l Abner*, and others. But topping them all was Harold Gray's *Little Orphan Annie*.

Although the *Annie* strip debuted in the prosperous 1920s, it exploded into its greatest popularity during the Depression-plagued 1930s. Without compromising the strip's appeal to kids, Gray began using it to comment on the hardscrabble, hard-times realities of the era, including unions, big business, political corruption, communism, and the New Deal. A radio show debuted in 1930 and film adaptations were produced in 1932 by RKO and in 1938 by Paramount.

In 1937, Pressman used Annie and her dog Sandy to brand its *"Orphan Annie" Bubble Pipe and Soap* set. It was a perfect example of a simple, traditional toy given a facelift and vitamin shot via a character license. Annie and her dog figured only on the colorful box. The pipe was a generic bubble pipe – albeit a very nice one, with an enameled wooden bowl, a metal stem, and a wooden mouthpiece, all packaged neatly with a cake of bubble soap.

Another media phenomenon of the 1930s was the Dionne Quintuplets. Born two months premature, on May 28, 1934, in Corbeil, a village on the outskirts of Callander, Ontario, Canada, the quints were very big, very happy news in possibly the darkest year of the Depression.

It is estimated that quintuplets occur only once in

about sixty million births. Such births at least come close to qualifying as miracles, and the media covered the Dionnes exhaustively for years. Every birthday renewed media interest in the Dionne quints, and *Life* magazine ran a cover story, "Going on Three," on May 17, 1937, eleven days before the children's third birthday.

That year, Pressman featured a *Quintuplet Embroidery Set*, with "ten colored dresses for embroidering," sized to fit the five "pretty 3½" decorated bisque dolls" included in the set. True, the name "Dionne" does not appear anywhere on the box. But with one-in-sixty-million odds, it really didn't have to.

LEFT
The Dionne Quintuplets monopolized the headlines through much of the 1930s.

RIGHT
J. Pressman produced quintuplets of its own in 1937 – five 3½-inch bisque dolls.

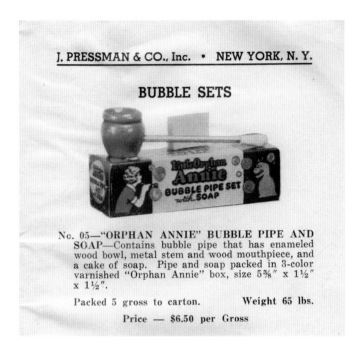

J. PRESSMAN & CO., Inc. • NEW YORK, N. Y.

BUBBLE SETS

No. 05—"ORPHAN ANNIE" BUBBLE PIPE AND
SOAP—Contains bubble pipe that has enameled
wood bowl, metal stem and wood mouthpiece, and
a cake of soap. Pipe and soap packed in 3-color
varnished "Orphan Annie" box, size 5⅜" x 1½"
x 1½".

Packed 5 gross to carton.   Weight 65 lbs.

Price — $6.50 per Gross

J. PRESSMAN & CO., Inc. • NEW YORK, N. Y.
SNOW WHITE CRAYON SET
(Continued)

No. 4226—SNOW WHITE CRAYON SET—Contains
24 assorted colored crayons, appealing black and
white, Snow White and dwarf pictures and one
colored picture, all set up in a beautifully designed and attractively colored lithographed box,
size 9¼" x 15⅜" x 1⅛".
Packed 4 doz. to carton.   Weight 42 lbs.
Price — $36.00 per Gross

TOP
Little Orphan Annie got a bubble pipe set in 1937.

BOTTOM
The *Snow White Crayon Set* featured in the 1938
catalog encouraged kids to take the Disney characters
home with them.

Toys of Disney's Celluloid World

Whereas the story of the Dionne Quintuplets felt like a fairytale brought to life, Walt Disney brought a fairytale to the silver screen. At Christmastime 1937, his studio, already a high-rolling media player thanks to Mickey Mouse, released its breakthrough feature-length cartoon, *Snow White and the Seven Dwarfs*. The product of four labor-intensive years at a cost of 1.5 million Depression-era dollars (three times over budget), it was universally mocked as "Disney's Folly." When the numbers for 1938 came in, however, *Snow White* emerged as the year's most successful picture, and by May 1939 it had grossed $6.5 million, making it the most profitable sound movie made to that date.

It seemed that every merchant and manufacturer on the good green planet wanted to license a piece of it, and Pressman was no exception. The same company whose 1937 catalog had offered such imitations of real life as *Little Mother's Laundry Set* and the *Luncheon Sets* now featured in its 1938 catalog four Snow White items.

This was truly big-time licensing, as Pressman joined arms simultaneously with Disney, Hollywood, and the much-beloved fairytale Disney had taken to the big screen. The toy company did not attempt to compete with Disney's cinematic achievement by creating some elaborate imitation of the world of Snow White, the Seven Dwarfs, the Handsome Prince, and the Evil Queen, but instead used Snow White and the other figures merely to brand two levels of crayon boxes and two levels of more elaborate crayon sets.

In one respect, this strategy was typical of the company at the time: make a familiar, generic plaything special by associating it with something sensational, current, and beloved. Yet the Disney Snow White license was even more strategic. Crayons engage a child's creative imagination. Here was an offering that combined these tools of the imagination with images of a fantastic fairytale realm born of imagination itself. Modest as a toy, it was a potion more powerful than even Walt Disney.

LEFT
Lotto, introduced in the 1937 catalog, was a variation on bingo.

RIGHT
Flash was a way of turning a simple top into a whole game.

ANAGRAMS

NEW YORK, N.Y. Made in U.S.A. No. 4031

& CO., INC.

Anagrams, 1945.

Chapter 4
Toys, Games, and WWII
1939–1945

World War II made a dramatic impact on consumers as well as the industries that served them. The Great Depression taught Americans to be frugal and drove industry to conserve costly materials, but the war brought this to a whole new level. Food, gasoline, and materials critical to the war effort were rigorously rationed by a federal War Production Board.

The toy industry was not immune to regulation. But, thanks to the lobbying efforts of the Toy Manufacturers of America (today simply called the Toy Association), the toy industry was classified as "essential," so it was in no danger of being shuttered by the government. Nevertheless, on March 30, 1942, the War Production Board issued an order prohibiting the manufacture of toys containing more than 7 percent of their weight in iron, steel, zinc, or rayon (used for parachutes). "Manufacturers show ingenuity in developing new playthings made from non-critical materials," the industry trade journal *Playthings* reported in an April 1942 story.

Unsurprisingly, paper dolls, puzzles, and board games increased in popularity because they already used non-critical materials. But most toymakers had to scramble to find ways to make traditionally metal toys out of wood or paper.

"Combination boards" combined two board games on one two-sided board. These are from 1945.

Pressman Pushes a Winning Strategy

Jack Pressman realized that his company was ideally positioned in the new wartime environment. Pressman had been making toys and games from wood and paper since it had opened its doors. The company had developed long-standing relationships with sources of material and manufacture, and it was skilled in making these playthings attractive, distinctive, inexpensive, and durable. The result was that J. Pressman & Co. did not simply survive the war years, it prospered through them.

Growth became a winning strategy. Already holding the high ground when it came to making toys out of non-rationed materials, Jack Pressman led a remarkable expansion in the volume and variety of his company's offerings. Where, for example, *Hop Ching Checkers* was offered in four variations across two catalog pages in 1939, it came in eight versions across eight pages of the 1945 catalog. This included such innovations as combining *Chinese Checkers* with other games on a reversible board. One set offered "the new sensation," a card game called *Michigan Pool*; another included traditional checkers; and still another combined *Hop Ching* with *three* other games – *Michigan Pool*, checkers, and backgammon.

Bingo had required two catalog pages in 1939 but expanded to four in 1945. Modeling clay and embroidery sets exhibited the same two-to-four doubling, and paint sets also doubled, from three pages to six.

No. 780—DUCK PINS—Has 10 assorted colored highly enameled pins 5″ in height. 3 enameled wooden balls complete the set. All in an attractive lithograph labeled box, size 13¼″ x 12¼″ x 2″.

Packed 2 doz. to Carton.   Weight 65 lbs.

Price — $78.00 per Gross

F. O. B. New York

In 1939, *Ring Toss* variations occupied three pages, which grew to five by 1945. *Duck Pins*, confined to a single page in 1939, commanded three in 1945. Table tennis exploded. Already popular in 1939, occupying five pages, in 1945 it sprawled over eight pages of catalog real estate.

Many consumer manufacturers, including some toymakers, shifted much or all production to goods for the war. But Pressman, neither equipped nor staffed to contribute its production capacity to the war effort, turned all its energy to supplying toys and games to the home front.

Duck Pins were a staple of the Pressman line for many years.

LEFT
Duck Pins in the 1939 catalog.

RIGHT
Duck Pins set from the 1950s.

A Growth in Sophistication

Jack Pressman's wartime approach did not rest solely on volume and variety. Under his leadership, marketing became more sophisticated. The catalog grew from a pamphlet of sixty-one pages in 1939 to a book of over a hundred pages in 1945. Where the 1939 catalog was printed in black and white on pulp stock with tiny, crudely reproduced illustrations, the 1945 edition featured two-color printing (black and orange) with larger and much better photographs of the merchandise displayed in clean, uncluttered layouts. The title page of the 1945 edition *spoke* to merchandisers and shopkeepers and did so eloquently. "All for You," the copy proclaimed:

> We present a comprehensive
> Line of STAPLE
> TOYS AND GAMES
> • To cater to the moods and talents of every child
> • To favor the purse strings of every parent
> • And to entitle YOU to PROFITS.

This was not a merchant simply hawking his wares. It was a thoughtful company treating children as individuals with unique "moods" and "talents," appealing to the financial realities their parents struggled to manage, and offering itself to retailers as a partner in profit. That the child figured at the top of the firm's value proposition says much about Jack Pressman's priorities. The war created a demand for entertainment, for escape, for something to give children the right to be children, and the Pressman company intended to support that right.

1939 New York World's Fair

The World's Fair opened in New York on April 30, 1939, five months before World War II began in Europe and nearly three years before the Pearl Harbor attack on December 7, 1941, thrust America into the war. The fair's slogan was "Dawn of a New Day," and the theme — for the first time in a world's fair — was a celebration of the future. The Great Depression was becoming a thing of the past, and the outlook, at least in the United States, was optimistic. Few Americans were convinced that the entire world was on the brink of war.

Whatever else a world's fair is, it is an opportunity for marketing, and, war or no war, the fair lasted two full seasons, from 1939 to 1940, drawing during its long run some forty-four million visitors. As Pressman had done in 1938 with Disney's sensational *Snow White and the Seven Dwarfs*, the company took full advantage of the marketing opportunity by licensing key imagery. The ubiquitous icon of the fair — the image that conveyed its unique brand — was the combination of the Trylon and Perisphere.

The Trylon was a lofty 610-foot-high spire connected to the Perisphere, 180 feet in diameter, by what was at the time the world's longest escalator. The Trylon and Perisphere were reproduced by the millions on a wide range of promotional materials, from postage stamps to commemorative plates. Pressman featured the Trylon and Perisphere on four new toys for 1939. There were three *World's Fair Paint Sets*, each in a "highly colored lithograph labeled box" featuring the Trylon and Perisphere as well as other evocations of the fair. In addition, Pressman offered a "World's Fair Ring Toss . . . made in replica of the World's Fair theme. In wood, highly finished, a white trylon and a white perisphere are the targets, mounted on a 12″ square wooden base."

J. PRESSMAN & CO., Inc. • NEW YORK, N. Y.

WORLD'S FAIR PAINT SET

No. 4220—WORLD'S FAIR PAINT SET—Contains 13 paints, 4 crayons, 2 water pans, a large camel's hair brush, 4 black and white World's Fair pictures to be painted, and a large sized, authentically shaped, wooden artist's palette, in a natural finish. All laid out attractively on a printed platform, set up in a highly colored lithograph labeled box, size 14⅜″ x 9⅜″ x 1¼″.

Packed 4 doz. to Carton.   Weight 48 lbs.

Price — $36.00 per Gross

No. 4223—WORLD'S FAIR PAINT SET—Contains authentically shaped 8½″ x 6½″ stained wooden artist's palette. Has 30 paint tablets, 2 complete boxes of assorted colored crayons, a large camel's hair brush, 2 water pans, 3 black and white large World's Fair pictures to be painted, and a large colored picture. This box is attractively designed and brightly lithographed, size 16¾″ x 12¼″.

Packed 2 doz. to Carton.   Weight 38 lbs.

Price — $72.00 per Gross

F. O. B. New York

[30]

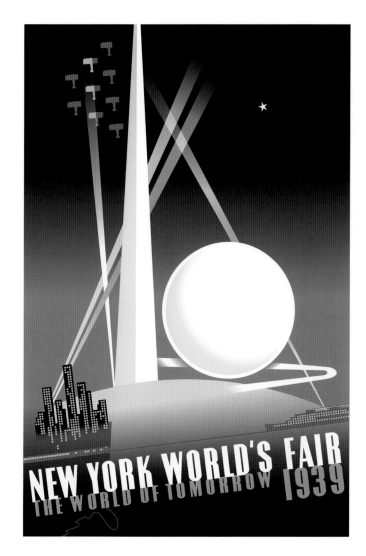

LEFT
The *World's Fair Paint Sets* made full use of the iconic imagery of the big show in New York, 1939.

RIGHT
Joseph Binder's poster for the World's Fair, featuring the Trylon and Perisphere.

42

J. PRESSMAN & CO., Inc. ● NEW YORK, N. Y.

BANG BIRD

No. 225—"BANG BIRD"—This set has two large paddles with enameled handles and bird. All in box, size 13¾" x 6¾" x 1⅜".

Packed 6 doz. to carton.   Weight 50 lbs.

Price — $36.00 per Gross

F. O. B. New York

[2]

J. PRESSMAN & CO., Inc. ● NEW YORK, N. Y.

TRICKY STICKS

No. 6—TRICKY STICKS—Contains seventeen 7½" sticks smoothly finished, with vari-colored end stripings set-up in an attractive printed cylindrical box 8¼" x 1⅝". Set comes complete with instructions.

Packed 24 doz. to carton.   Weight 38 lbs.

Price — $16.00 per Gross

No. 24—TRICKY STICKS—Contains forty-one 7½" sticks smoothly finished with vari-colored end stripings set-up in an attractive cylindrical box, 8¼" x 2". Set comes complete with instructions.

Packed 12 doz. to carton.   Weight 36 lbs.

Price — $36.00 per Gross

F. O. B. New York

[60]

As with 1938's *Snow White* crayon sets, the idea was to offer a traditional toy made special by decorating it with images of an event that sparked the popular imagination. Other than the paint sets and ring toss game, however, most of the offerings for 1939 were simple, traditional playthings, some offered in a choice of standard or deluxe versions. Pastimes such as bingo, *Bang a Peg*, *Bang Bird* — a uniquely named variation on badminton — and *Tricky Sticks* (pick-up sticks) dwelled in a world far apart from the World's Fair, let alone the prospect of a world war.

Pressman offered an updated version of the fishing games that had been introduced back in 1932 and would resurface again and again, right up to the present. True, there were two wooden soldier sets in the 1939 catalog, but these were classic "toy soldiers," fit for a march to *Babes in Toyland*, not to battle. Much the same can be said about *Army and Navy Ten-Pins*, one of four ten-pins games offered in 1939. The pins may have been painted to look like soldiers and sailors, but they were nothing more or less than painted wooden pins waiting to be knocked down. There was no attempt at realism. These were toys, belonging to the world of children's play, not the increasingly dark world of impending conflict.

Traditional playthings offered in the 1939 catalog.

LEFT
Bang Bird was a uniquely named variation on badminton.

RIGHT
Tricky Sticks, a version of pick-up sticks, is a classic game of dexterity and patience.

43

LEFT
Pegs was a simple yet
extraordinarily versatile game of
the 1930s.

RIGHT
An innovative word game
especially for children, 1945.

NO. 1501 BOMB THE NAVY

J. PRESSMAN & CO., INC. NEW YORK

This set consists of three formidable looking men-of-war, printed on heavy paper, with detachable wooden bases, a wood cannon, and 3 wood pellets of ammunition. All in an attractive, lithograph labeled setup box, size 6⅝″ x 6⅝″ x 1½″.

Packed:
12 Dozen to Carton
Weight: 58 lbs.
Price:
$16.00 per Gross

[11]

GAME OF INDIA NO. 3162

J. PRESSMAN & CO., INC. NEW YORK

An interesting game guaranteed to promote entertainment when put to use. The game consists of a highly colored, elaborately designed platform, a pair of celluloid dice, an assortment of vari-colored wooden discs, a cylindrical cardboard shaker, and instructions. The lithograph labeled box encasing the game, size 13¾″ x 10⅞″ x 1½″, is carried out in a vivid, artistically worthy Indian jungle motif.

Packed:
4 Dozen to Carton
Weight: 40 lbs.
Price:
$36.00 per Gross

[34]

War? *What* War?

The 1945 catalog includes but one explicitly martial item, *Bomb the Navy*, essentially "three formidable looking men-of-war" — a battleship, aircraft carrier, and submarine — "printed on heavy paper" and meant to stand upright on wooden bases. A wooden cannon with a rubber band launched "wood pellets of ammunition" at the two-dimensional vessels.

As a stylized echo of war, the toy was far from realistic and was thus a pastime of peace, as harmless as the other offerings for 1945.

These toys included, for the first time in Pressman's history, what became a classic combination: a two-sided game board, checkers on one side, backgammon on the other. Another first was *Game of India*, a knockoff of *Parcheesi*, which was introduced in America in 1867 by the newly founded E. G. Selchow & Co. and had been selling well ever since.

Pressman's version was an example of a common practice in the toy industry of making what were somewhat euphemistically called "parallel" products. Jack Pressman became a master of copying success and then making it either better or cheaper than the original — and sometimes both. Not that the Selchow version was truly original, since *this* "game of India" really had originated in India, where it had been played since the Middle Ages.

LEFT
Surprisingly, *Bomb the Navy* was the only military-themed toy in the 1945 catalog. It featured "a wood cannon and 3 wood pellets of ammunition."

RIGHT
Game of India brought a touch of the exotic to Pressman's board game offerings in 1945 and was a "game guaranteed to promote entertainment when put to use."

Assorted Fun and the
Beginning of the End of an Era

The two signature merchandising presentations of 1945 were the spectacular — and spectacularly inexpensive — *Big 10 Assortment* and *Big 25 Package Assortment*.

Call these the Whitman Samplers of the toy industry. The Big 10 was an assortment of a dozen of Pressman's "best 10c retailers . . . each number . . . built to the high specifications required by our trade, and each consequently [containing] value to the hilt." The Big 25 kicked things up a notch by offering an assortment of twelve "of our choice 25c retailers." The catalog copy explained: "Each and every item in this assortment, beyond the beauty of its art work and colorful packaging, possesses an intrinsic fullness destined to insure increased assortment sales."

The assortments may be seen as celebrations of the company's timeless playthings, islands of innocence and security in a very turbulent, fast-changing, and menacing era. The 1945 catalog featured the latest version of the venerable *Zellophone*, which had been introduced not long after the company opened its doors, and it also offered the bubble sets and marbles that have been a part of childhood, it would seem, forever.

But "forever" is a long, long time, especially in the toy business.

Paper and wood did not just save Pressman during World War II, they drove the company's prosperity.

Paper and wood had been the go-to materials for this toymaker since it started making its own toys. But now another material, waiting in the wings, was about to make its entrance in a big way.

The first manmade plastic, Parkesine, was patented in England in 1856, and through the late nineteenth century and well into the twentieth, it evolved into Bakelite and then a variety of other plastics. World War II spurred development of plastics used in many military applications, especially in such things as cockpit canopies and windshields for aircraft. When the war ended, civilian industries inherited a cutting-edge technology that made instantly available a vast and growing range of inexpensive plastics capable of being molded into practically anything.

Jack had a well-deserved reputation as a man of impeccable taste, whether it was in the clothes he wore or the general tidiness he demanded. He would pick up paper clips and empty ashtrays in the office. Also notable were his astuteness and wide-ranging real-world knowledge, which consistently allowed him to best the competition at auctions, no matter what was being gaveled — whether antiques, fine arts, or factory machinery. At this point, with peace returned to the nation, Jack Pressman had a vision of the future. In 1947 he bought a piece of brand-new equipment, an injection molding machine, and the very first thing he made with it was bingo balls. Not of wood, but of plastic.

FOLLOWING PAGES
The 1945 catalog featured assortments of popular games conveniently packaged to sell for retailers.

46

BIG 10 ASSORTMENT

•

An unsurpassable assortment, containing 12 of our best 10c retailers. Each number is built to the high specifications required by our trade, and each consequently contains value to the hilt. Each and every item in this assortment, beyond the beauty of its art work and colorful packaging, possesses an intrinsic fullness destined to insure increased assortment sales.

The assortment is packed 6 dozen to a corrugated shipping carton; 6 pieces each of 12 numbers; and weighs 28 lbs.

Price: $16.00 per Gross

BIG 25 PACKAGE ASSORTMENT

An incomparable assortment comprised of 12 of our choice 25c retailers Each number is built to the high specifications required by our trade, and each consequently contains value to the hilt. Each and every item in this assortment, beyond the beauty of its art work and colorful packaging, possesses an intrinsic fullness destined to insure increased assortment sales.

The assortment is packed 4 doz. to a corrugated shipping carton; 4 pieces of each of 12 numbers and weighs 45 lbs.

Price: $39.00 per Gross

Lynn Rambach
as a stylish young
professional.

Chapter 5
Jack and Lynn:
A Love Story

1942–1959

From 1922, when the company was incorporated, through the opening years of World War II, J. Pressman & Co. was all about Jack Pressman. In 1941, Jack was introduced to someone who would begin to change that.

Jack Pressman was a widower—his wife having died from cancer—when his friends Sophie and Moe Lane introduced him to Sophie's sister Lynn Rambach. Lynn, whose birth certificate called her Lillian, was a twenty-nine-year-old beauty known for her stylish manner of dress, always punctuated by what today would be called "statement" hats, which were something of a personal trademark with her.

She worked in the retail fashion industry, having gotten her start in 1929, when she took a streetcar to the Abraham & Strauss department store in response to an ad in the *Brooklyn Eagle* for a secretary. It was at the very start of the Great Depression, and when she entered the A&S office, she found it

jammed with applicants for the one job. Deciding it was a hopeless proposition, she turned on her heel, walked out the door, and got on another streetcar. When she realized she was heading in the wrong direction, she took it as a sign to return to the store. She got the job and immediately made the most of it, taking every opportunity to assist in A&S fashion shows. By 1935, she was the manager of feature publicity for the company and was subsequently promoted to fashion director.

Becoming a successful career woman during the Great Depression was no small achievement, but Lynn had also taken some hard knocks. She was married to a husband with a roving eye, and, not surprisingly, the

50

TOP
Lynn and Jack dining out.

BOTTOM LEFT
Six sisters and the one brother:
Gertrude, Norma, Sadie, Marvin,
Sophie, and May. Lynn is on the far
right.

BOTTOM CENTER
Lynn and Jack on the beach.

BOTTOM RIGHT
Jack with his brothers-in-law (*left
to right*): Izzy, Sam, Harry, Moe, and
Marvin. Jack is second from right.

marriage ended in divorce in 1939. Sophie and Moe always looked out for Lynn and, with Jack recently widowed, the pair indulged in a little matchmaking.

Jack was smitten, and Lynn was charmed, but the difference in their ages concerned her. She was twenty-nine, and he was forty-six. In the end, Lynn, thoroughly modern woman though she was, consulted a fortune teller, who told her, in effect, to get over it and embrace her destiny. Liberated from doubt, her love for Jack blossomed, and they married in 1942. Jack was welcomed into the large Rambach family, in which Lynn was one of seven siblings, six sisters and one brother. He, in turn, immediately adopted Lynn's daughter, Ann, as his own.

Family Life

For both, it was a second marriage, yet Jack nevertheless became the love of Lynn's life and vice versa. It did not hurt that he lavished gifts on his bride, and on their honeymoon they conceived a son, Edward. For both, this was a welcome surprise. One of the things Jack had made a point of telling Lynn before they talked marriage was that he believed he could not have children. He was clearly mistaken. A second son, James, was born six years later.

Through the war years, Lynn – no stranger to business – contented herself with making a home for Jack, their firstborn, and Ann, but it may be that she began to insinuate her sense of style and design into the company during the early 1940s. The 1945 catalog is radically different in appearance from the earlier publications. It uses a splash of color, has much improved photographs of the toys, devotes more space to each item, and even pays attention to typography and layout. In short, the catalog is *designed*, and well-designed at that. In an interview she gave when she was ninety-five, Lynn commented, "I truly brought fashion to the toy business." In her opinion, "Everything they were doing there [at Pressman] was corny." She made it her mission to introduce the company to high style: "Our boxes became chicer and people knew we had taste."

TOP LEFT
Jack, Lynn, Ann, Ed, and Jim on vacation at the historic Hollywood Beach Hotel, Florida.

TOP RIGHT
Jack with his sons, Ed and Jim, ready to party in Florida.

BOTTOM
Ed Pressman in front of a company vehicle outside the factory in East Paterson, New Jersey.

TOP
Lynn and Jack in action at the 1107 Broadway showroom.

BOTTOM
The custom-built "He-and-She" desk at 1107 Broadway, March 1953.

OPPOSITE
Promoting "new ideas in Dr. and Nurse Kits" with highly theatrical ads in two 1955 issues of *Playthings*.

Lynn Makes Her Move

In 1925, Jack had partnered with Max Eibetz, who ran the company's Brooklyn factory located on Carroll Street. Around 1947, after what she recalled (in a 2007 interview for *The Toy Book*) as "much conversation," Lynn persuaded her husband to buy out Eibetz's half of the business to make room for her. When Eibetz refused either to sell his half or buy Jack's, Jack presided over the dissolution of the partnership, with each man taking a part of the business. Jack then reincorporated J. Pressman & Co. as Pressman Toy Corp., naming Lynn vice president and moving the company's factory to the Marcal Building in East Paterson, New Jersey — though they would later move back to Brooklyn, at Bush Terminal.

Lynn embraced Jack as a mentor, remarking in 2007 that he "was a wonderful salesperson. I certainly did learn from him." With uncharacteristically self-deprecating modesty, she claimed that all she knew how to do was "to be fun, charming, and glamorous."

In fact, she was good at selling, maybe *too* good. "I'll never forget one time I was waiting on a customer and Jack called me into the office. It was the first time he scolded me." He told her, "Lynn, you were so enthusiastic that you sold a man merchandise he couldn't use in ten years. That's the worst thing you can do." At the time, her husband's criticism reduced her to tears, but she soon realized that he had taught her a secret of the company's longevity: "You've got to know your customer."

For her part, Lynn delivered tremendous value to Pressman, bringing to it — and the entire toy industry, really — her knowledge and experience of fashion and design. To begin with, she redesigned the company's packaging, and later brought in an ad agency from the fashion industry to produce Pressman's first television commercial.

What are the Pressmans up to this year?

If you've heard rumors...they're TRUE! Pressman's new ideas in DR. and NURSE KITS make everything else obsolete. Don't sign an order until you've seen them!

**ressman** TOY CORPORATION

1107 Broadway, New York 10, N. Y.

What's new?

Plenty at Pressman!

There's been a minor revolution going on behind that screen. You're going to see a line of Dr. and Nurse toys that makes everything you've seen obsolete. You'll see a line-up of 78 new items including famous name toys that will make your eyes pop. You'll see a TV promotion "spectacular" that will pre-sell every youngster in America! And remember last year's Pressman "haven for dog-tired buyers"? Well, you'll have the surprise of your life when you see what we have dreamed up for your comfort this year when you visit the Toy Fair. Yes, be doubly sure to make Pressman your *first* stop.

**ressman** TOY CORPORATION

1107 Broadway, New York 10, N. Y.

ABOVE
Jack and Lynn go full
P. T. Barnum, January 1956.

RIGHT
The Pressman sales force in
1957, including Lynn's nephew
Norman Oshin.

Lynn told an interviewer that when she became Pressman's vice president, the "toy industry had no fashion sense at all." Little wonder, since women executives were virtually unknown in the industry, except for those involved in dolls. Her personal flair — the fun, the charm, the glamour — was attractive to the overwhelmingly male world of buyers and wholesalers. Adorned in her trademark hats, she brought a distinctive flamboyance and excitement to the company, which complemented Jack's business sense and sales expertise.

In February 1953, the industry magazine *Playthings* credited Lynn with what it called Pressman's new "distinctive designs." She told the magazine, "Jack Pressman, my boss, gives me an unlimited budget for packaging because, being a lover of art himself, he firmly believes it is never too early to have children become familiar with what embodies good taste, and what is good in art."

Calling her husband her "boss" said more about 1950s business culture than it did about the reality of the couple's business relationship. Both legally and functionally, they were business partners, a relationship they symbolized in the sleek new showroom Pressman opened at 1107 Broadway in Manhattan. The couple shared an elegant private office, dominated by a massive "He-and-She" desk, which had been custom-built for the president and vice president in a gently curved crescent. Jack sat at one end, Lynn at the other, so that they faced both outward and slightly toward one another, presenting themselves to their guests as perfect equals in business.

Putting More Family in a Family Business

As leadership of Pressman Toy Corp. was now divided between the couple, Lynn brought in a number of members of her family to run aspects of operations. Her nephew Norman Oshin came in as sales manager in 1947 and, by 1957, would rise to vice president in charge of sales. Norman's brother Shelly ran the factory. Another nephew, Bobby Lane, owned the box company that began supplying all the newly designed boxes for Pressman Toy.

Other relatives came in as well. Jack and Lynn also spent many summer weekends on the terrace at Moe and Sophie Lane's apartment. They weren't just soaking up the sun. The toymakers did not miss an opportunity to recruit the Lanes (or anyone else who happened to be visiting) to help Pressman with subassembly work, such as putting pegs or checkers into bags. Every minute and every penny counted.

Pressman Celebrates 35th Year in the Toy Business

Front—Herb Cadel, Jack Pressman, George Gossert. In back—Dave Feldman, Fred Kroll, Norm Oshin, Phil Seltzer.

An Atmosphere of Celebration

As Lynn was instrumental in expanding the company as a *family* company, she also extended the concept of "family" to much of the industry. Stakeholders from outside the company — the buyers, merchandisers, jobbers, vendors, and industry journalists with whom Pressman Toy had relationships — were brought closer to the company through the atmosphere of fun and celebration Lynn fostered.

In the fashion world, Lynn had enjoyed creating lavish fashion shows. Now she specialized in transforming promotional events at the annual Toy Fair and other shows into parties to which everyone doing business with Pressman was welcomed as a member of the extended family.

Because she and Jack were running a toy company, the party themes were typically playful and included lavish costumes.

ABOVE
Jack and Lynn enjoying themselves at themed costume parties. The man in top hat and checked suit, seated next to Jack, is Paul Schoenstein, the Pulitzer Prize–winning managing editor of the *New York Journal-American*.

LEFT
Jack and Lynn on the terrace of Sophie and Moe Lane's Manhattan apartment.

March 22, 1955
5:00 P.M.

Dear "J.P." -

Norman just called from Pennsylvania and he is all excited --
business is terrific!

From Fred: Norm worked with Klein Brothers in Allentown..
This account is now in the Lodge Book. They gave Norm an
order for $5100, which is terrific....Also, B & B Sales in
Allentown gave him an order for about $2500 to start. He has
been dashing back and forth between Allentown and Lancaster
to keep his dates -- soaking wet, but he is very happy because
business is great. Norm says he is doing better selling
"Stumblebum" and "Home" without the samples -- and I can
see why... For a lousy territory like Pennsylvania, I think he
is doing a terrific job. Much better than I used to do when I
covered Pennsylvania..... (Fred)

From your F. W... I just came back from seeing Syd Rubin at
NBC and I met there with Paul Winchell. I might make this
"Stumblebum" game a Paul Winchell game.

IF YOU LOVE ME (this is from your F. W.), you will remember
not to eat any sugar or salt...You will go in to see the chef,
give him a $10 bill and let him cater to you. If he wont, leave
the damn place and go to another place. I implore you -- as much
as you love Larry, do what I ask you first. It is because I love
you and Larry that I ask you this.

Tune in tomorrow to hear this exciting chapter of -- "The Office
Wife." --- Will J. P. eat sugar and salt? -- Will the chef at
the Fontaine Bleau cater to J.P? -- If not, will the chef give
J.P. his $10.00 back? -- Will J. P. leave F. W. for L. L.?
Tune in tomorrow so as not to miss the answers to these impor-
tant questions on your favorite program -- "The Office Wife."

            Love, love, love,
            and kisses --

            Your F. W.

March 23, 1955

Dear "JP" --

Today is a lovely but windy day -- perfect for
you to be in Florida.

I got a call from Bob Silverman and am going
out to the warehouse this afternoon to see if
it is either "yes" or "no."

Tonight I am going to see the show "Cat on the
Hot Tin Roof." If it is good, I will let you know
so that you can go to see it when you come home.

The main reason I am writing you today is to
nag you, and remind you, and nag you again to
eat the right food and keep the right hours --
Don't dare let anyone influence you into knocking
yourself out. Be in bed by 10 -- sleep late --
and sleep for two hours in the afternoon. I mean
it, I mean it, I mean it. So for God's sakes,
listen to me.

The children are wonderful and everything is
just fine...

            Yours for
            a million more years...

March 25, 1955

Dear "JP" --

    I'm busy...

        I love you...

            Your F. W.

Letters from Lynn to an ailing Jack, taking it easy
in Florida as she took charge in New York.

"I'm Busy ... I Love You ...
Your F. W."

The love story of Jack and Lynn Pressman, as well as the story of what had become *their* company, entered a new phase in 1953, when Jack began to suffer the increasingly debilitating effects of heart disease.

As Lynn looked after her husband, she also began to take over more of the company's operations. When Jack took a convalescent vacation at Miami Beach's Hotel Fontainebleau in March 1955, hoping to recoup at least some of his health, Lynn did more and more of the daily legwork of the business. She made a point of keeping her husband informed with letters chock-full of crystal-clear business details leavened with the banter of a loving wife to a loving husband. The missives were addressed to "J. P." from "F. W.," which was shorthand for what Jack called Lynn: Fabulous Wife.

A letter dated March 22, 1955, 5:00 p.m., reports on the performance of Pressman sales reps in Allentown and Lancaster – how "Norm worked with Klein Brothers in Allentown" and got "an order for $5100, which is terrific," and how he "has been dashing back and forth between Allentown and Lancaster to keep his dates – soaking wet, but he is very happy because business is great." She conveys a message from the sales manager: "For a lousy territory like Pennsylvania, I think he is doing a terrific job."

Lynn goes on to report that she herself "just came back from seeing Syd Rubin at NBC and I met there with Paul Winchell." Winchell was the human half of a phenomenally popular TV ventriloquist act,

"Paul Winchell and Jerry Mahoney," and she wrote her husband that she might make their new *Stumblebum* game "a Paul Winchell game."

From business, she turned to another matter: "IF YOU LOVE ME (this is from your F. W.), you will remember not to eat any sugar or salt.... You will go in to see the chef, give him a $10 bill and let him cater to you. If he wont, leave the damn place and go to another place." With this, she closed, inviting him to "Tune in tomorrow to hear this exciting chapter of – 'The Office Wife.' – Will J. P. eat sugar and salt? – Will the chef at the Fontaine Bleau cater to J. P.? – If not, will the chef give J. P. his $10.00 back?" And she signed off with "Love, love, love, and kisses – Your F. W."

The next day brought another letter, beginning "Today is a lovely but windy day – perfect for you to be in Florida." She had a brief business message but announced that her "main reason" for writing "is to nag you, and remind you, and nag you again to eat the right food and keep the right hours.... Be in bed by 10 – sleep late – and sleep for two hours in the afternoon. I mean it, I mean it, I mean it. So for God's sakes, listen to me." She signed off with "The children are wonderful and everything is just fine ... Yours for a million more years ..."

There are more letters, but the most touching, perhaps, is the one dated March 25, 1955:

Dear "JP" –
      I'm busy ...
           I love you ...
                Your F. W.

Zellophone

pressman toy corp., new york, n.y. — made in u.s.a. — 1108

The *Zellophone* went plastic in
1949 and stayed that way.

Chapter 6
Plastics

1947–1953

Page 15 of the 1949 Pressman Toy Corporation catalog featured a bingo game. Nothing new about this. Bingo had long been a Pressman staple. But the new listing boasted of "printed and embossed plastic numbers." The word *plastic* leaps out.

In 1947 Jack Pressman bought an injection molding machine. Capable of turning out any number of toys and parts of toys out of plastic, the machine was first put to work making bingo balls out of the new material rather than the traditional wood, and then his company highlighted this innovation in the next year's catalog. Today, we may find it difficult to think of substituting plastic for wood as something to brag on, but Jack Pressman understood that plastic, which had been essential to many of the weapons of World War II – small parts, electronic parts, and large assemblies, such as aircraft windscreens, canopies, and turret "blisters" – was now available to civilian America. And American consumers were excited by it.

Plastic could be molded into almost any shape and with great detail, which made it a more versatile material for more and more varied toys. Molding plastic toys and toy parts was fast, and it was limited in quantity only by how much raw plastic was available. After the war, the floodgates were open. The ingredients of plastic were abundant enough to transform the postwar years into the Age of Plastic worldwide.

Indeed, the American consumer saw in plastics the modern world, a world of more variety, more colorful and appealing design, and lower cost. Jack Pressman's company was in the vanguard of toymakers who made the most out of the plastics revolution.

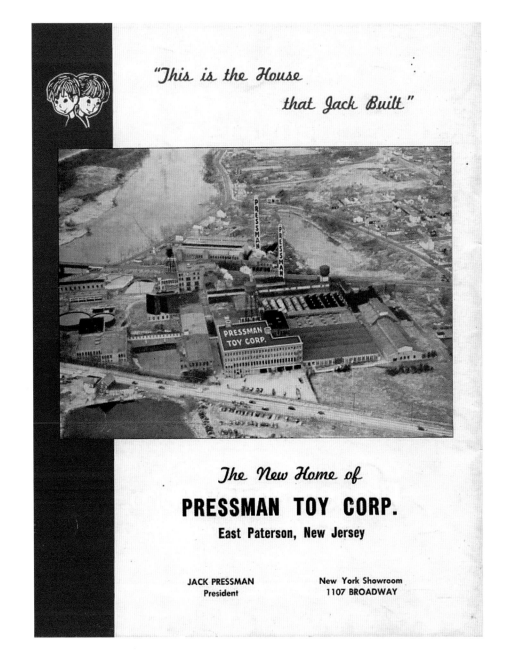

"This is the House that Jack Built"

The New Home of

PRESSMAN TOY CORP.

East Paterson, New Jersey

JACK PRESSMAN
President

New York Showroom
1107 BROADWAY

LEFT
The back cover of the 1951 catalog, featuring the new Pressman factory in East Paterson, New Jersey.

TOP RIGHT
Jack at a charity luncheon.

BOTTOM RIGHT
The spectacular new showroom at 1107 Broadway made the pages of *Playthings* in March 1952.

New Factory, New Showroom

As for getting up and running, Jack Pressman installed his molding machine in a now-vacant aircraft plant in East Paterson, New Jersey. Defense plants had sprouted like weeds in wartime America, and, after V-E and V-J Day, they were being sold to eager entrepreneurs at pennies on the dollar. The same catalog that featured the plastic bingo balls proudly advertised Pressman's new war-surplus manufacturing plant in a dramatic aerial shot.

That photograph also appeared in the March 1949 issue of *Playthings*, the principal periodical of the toy industry, in a story headlined "Pressman Toy Corporation Holds Annual Luncheon." The event was staged in the firm's new, spacious, and very modern showrooms at 1107 Broadway, a prestigious location connected by a skybridge to the Toy Building at 200 Fifth Avenue, site of the industry's annual Toy Fair.

Pressman Toy Corporation was now physically located at the industry's epicenter. A year earlier, in the February 1948 *Playthings*, Jack had declared, "The war years are over and now we are going to give the children the kind of toys that are due them." The March 1949 article reported, "In the short span of five months Jack Pressman produced more goods than he had done in any one of his previous thirty years as a manufacturer."

Examples of Early Pressman Plastics

Pressman may have forsaken wood for plastic, but he did not discard the toys themselves. The *Zellophone*, for instance, had appeared in the earliest Pressman catalogs during the 1920s. The 1949 catalog featured it, but now it was made with a large, boldly designed plastic frame. It looked like a brand-new toy. Other well-established Pressman staples also received plastic makeovers. The 1949 catalog featured the usual magic sets, fishing games, *Skill Ball* (formerly called *Bollo Ball*), and the ever-popular *Chinese Checkers*, but now with more plastic components.

Renewing traditional Pressman "staple" toys with plastic was consistent with the "Pledge" Jack Pressman published on page 1 of the company's 1950 catalog, in which he distilled the credo of the company's product line into a single sentence: "Our creative efforts have developed the finest line of staples on the market, augmented by constant adventures into exciting new specialty items." Traditional toys with proven appeal – "staples" – would never be supplanted by novel items but merely "augmented" by them. "This we have always done," Jack wrote. "This we will continue to do in increased measure."

Where these staples could be remade in plastic, they were. But when it came to marbles, glass still reigned supreme. Pages 28–29 of the 1949 catalog

A Pledge

As never before, we are aware of our responsibility as a source of supply for you. 35 years of experience has nurtured in us a fixed idea concerning those basic elements requisite for recognition as a dependable supplier.

Our creative efforts have developed the finest line of staples on the market, augmented by constant adventures into exciting new specialty items.

Of utmost importance, our prices are always aimed under the market — and we rarely miss, insuring you thereby that extra margin of profit.

Last, but far from least, our SERVICE is our banner. Sparing nothing, indulging every personal effort, with pride and with integrity, we deliver the goods.

This we have always done. This we will continue to do in increased measure.

Pressman

Jack's Pledge, 1950.

When Jack was the "Marble King,"
January 1953.

featured a vast array of aggies, alleys, red devils, cat's-eyes, and the like. Jack Pressman made sure his company would always be well supplied directly from its chief marble-making partner, Marble King, which today is still going strong in Paden, West Virginia. Pressman-branded Marble King products were so intimately identified with the Pressman firm that Jack himself was known throughout the toy industry as the "Marble King."

In a 2019 article published by the Woodhaven (Queens, NY) Cultural and Historical Society, either the article's author or Lynn Pressman (it is not clear) points out that Jack's "Marble King" nickname originated less in his company's success with marketing marbles than in the vast supplies of marbles he bought for the company's *Chinese Checkers* games. In 1950, these games were no longer marketed under the *Hop Ching* name but were now simply *Chinese Checkers*. Was this a nod to diversity, as *Hop Ching* rings as culturally insensitive to a contemporary American ear? Or was it a recognition that *Chinese Checkers* had assumed a prominent place in American pop culture, which made the *Hop Ching* moniker irrelevant? Perhaps it was a bit of both.

Fred Kroll

Fred Kroll, the *Hungry Hungry Hippos* Man

In 1947, Fred Kroll's father sold his business, the Novel Toy Company, a manufacturer of magnetic games, to Pressman Toy for $25,000. In 1951, after Fred got out of the army and was just married, he joined Pressman as a salesperson for $150 per week. Thanks to his success he received a nice raise year after year. "After six years," Fred related, "I asked Mr. Pressman if I could buy into his business, and he said, 'No, I have two boys and a girl.'"

But Fred went on to have a tremendously successful career in the industry. He was best known for creating the game *Trouble* for Kohner Bros. and for finding and licensing the game *Hungry Hungry Hippos* to Hasbro. Despite turning down Fred's bid to buy into Pressman Toy, Jack and the company continued to hold a special place in Fred's heart. Jack was his mentor, and Pressman was where Fred Kroll started his decades-long career.

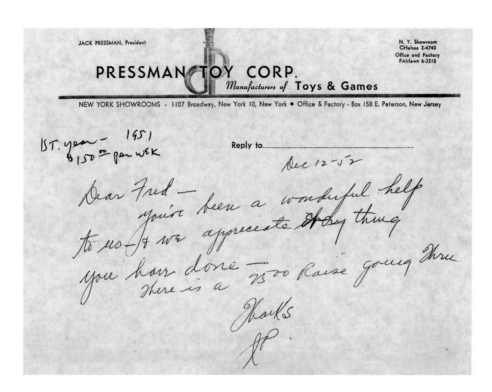

Fred Kroll worked his way up to eastern sales manager at Pressman before moving on to a long and distinguished career in the toy business.

64

Branding Becomes More Distinctive

As plastic took over in a vast range of industries, making it possible for more companies to turn out more goods more cheaply, the roles of branding and marketing became increasingly important across the entire consumer spectrum to distinguish each company's offerings.

Playthings reported that Pressman's March 4, 1949, annual luncheon "celebrated the first birthday of the Small Fry Kids," who appeared on the company's new logo. The Small Fry Kids were "two precocious youngsters" who "drew their first breath on New Year's day of 1948" and "thrived during that year."

OPPOSITE LEFT
Probably the first ad for Pressman in its new incarnation as Pressman Toy Corporation, March 1948.

OPPOSITE RIGHT
The *Small Fry Doctor and Nurse Bags* in the 1953 catalog.

RIGHT
Photo setup for *Small Fry Barber Set*, 1953. Young Jim Pressman wields the straight razor.

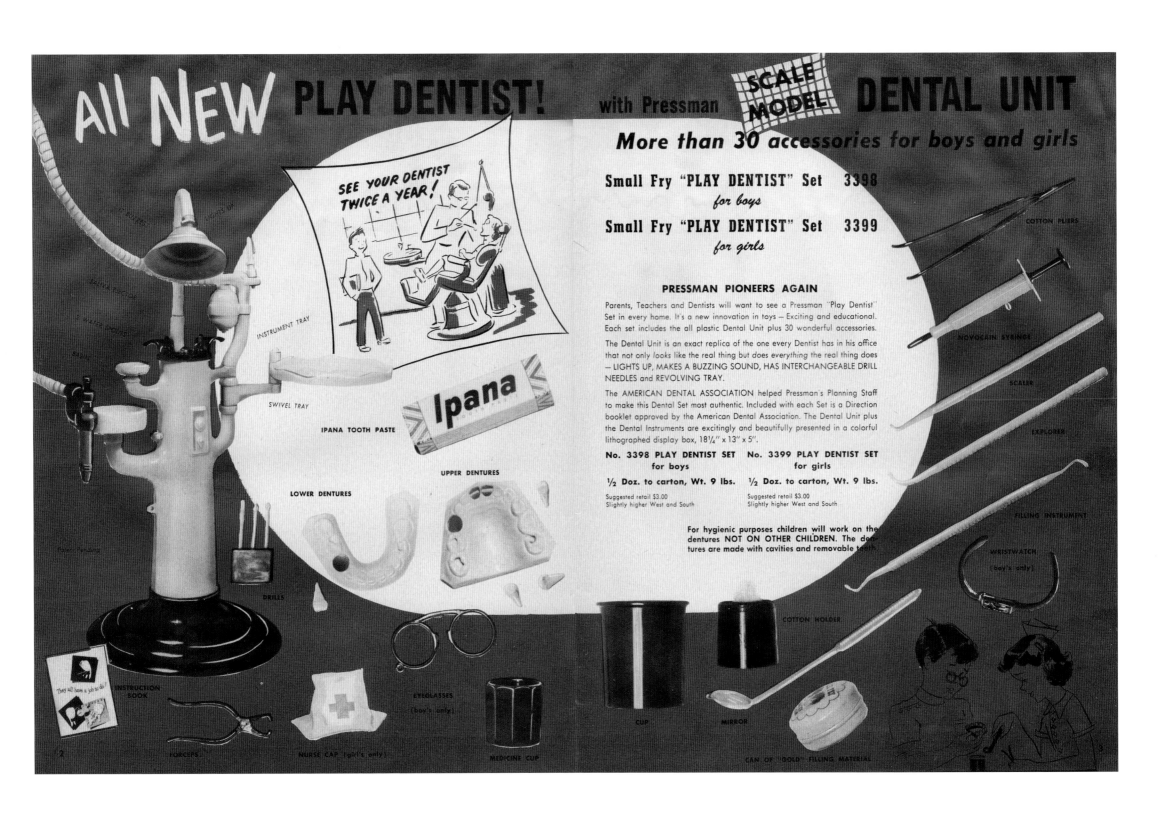

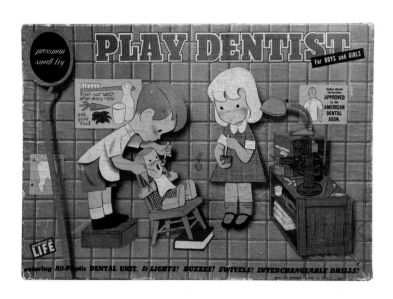

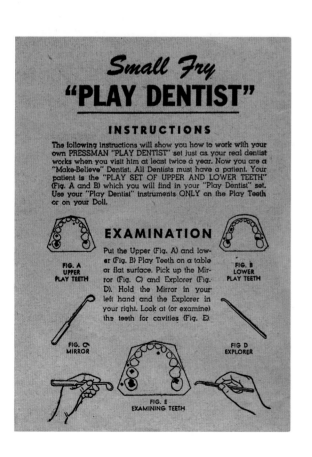

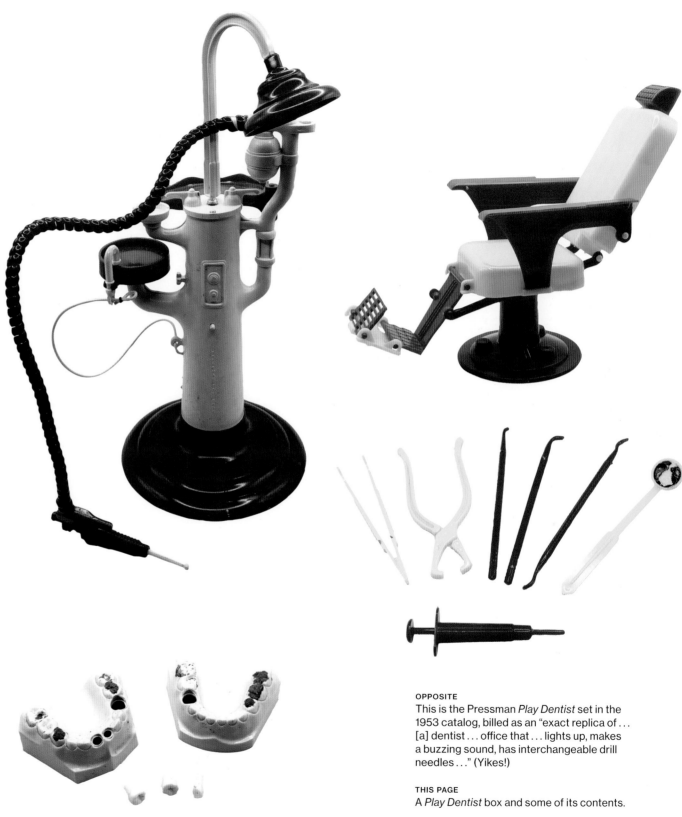

Lynn Pressman Makes Her Mark

Jack's wife, Lynn, was also coming very much into her own as part of the new postwar company. Personally stylish – always seen in one of her many trademark hats – she became increasingly active in giving the company's packaging, print advertising, and other aspects of marketing a distinctively stylish look, seen most vividly in the catalog covers and the presentation of the products themselves.

Her first major impact came in the form of new "Small Fry" doctor and nurse kits, which were prominently featured on pages 2 and 3 of the 1949 catalog. Page 1 was reserved for two *Small Fry Barber Sets*, the standard and the deluxe models. The standard model included a miniature Gem razor, paper Gem blades, shaving soap, a shaving bowl (interestingly, wooden rather than plastic), a bottle of Wildroot Hair Tonic, a shaving brush, comb, scissors, mustache, and "direction book." The deluxe version added to this a hand mirror, cutting comb, trimming comb, and some Aqua Velva aftershave lotion.

The story is that all three kits were inspired by the anxiety of Lynn and Jack's children, who all dreaded visits to the doctor. Young Jim Pressman was also initially shy of visits to the barber. Lynn reasoned that such fears were hardly unique to her children. She believed that many parents would see the toys as useful in helping their kids cope with their feelings.

The doctor and nurse kits evolved through the years. In 1951, leatherette (that is, plastic) doctor's and nurse's bags were added, inspired, according to the 2019 article from the Woodhaven Cultural and Historical Society, by Lynn's own recollections of doctors' house calls when she was a little girl growing up in the Woodhaven neighborhood.

The doctor, nurse, and barber sets were again featured, even more prominently, in the 1950 catalog, and in 1953, a new profession was added. In advance of the new toy's release, a "Secret Project" was teased to the toy industry in ads that announced the secret would be revealed on "D-Day." At last, an elaborate full-page ad published in the February 1953 *Playthings* proclaimed: "'D' day is HERE at Pressman."

It was the release of a *Small Fry Dentist Set* – or, as the ad put it, *"D"entist Set*. There were four versions, two for boys and two for girls. The sets had no fewer than thirty pieces each, among them a daunting array of appallingly pointy instruments, including a cotton pliers, "Novocain syringe," scaler, explorer, and filling instrument. There was a scary-looking "forceps" (i.e., pliers) for tooth extractions, not to mention a drill that lit up and buzzed. (It came with *three* interchangeable bits!) Also included was a set of "play dentures." "For hygienic purposes," the catalog copy explained, "children will work on the dentures NOT ON OTHER CHILDREN. The dentures are made with cavities and removable teeth."

In February of the following year, 1954, a new ad offered toy sellers a "Top Secret Formula for Success in '54." It looked like an equation but was (the ad announced) a "magic formula":

$$G_2D_5P_3 = \$$$

The ad promised that its magical meaning would be revealed at the upcoming Toy Fair, but, writing in his own voice, Jack Pressman dropped a big hint:

That FW* of mine gave you D-Day with the introduction of her Dentist Set last year. It was the fastest moving item PRESSMAN ever had in 31 years, of success. This year, I gave her the green

*fabulous wife

light and boy did she go! We are ready with 10 Lynn Pressman Originals . . . all set for the Toy Fair. Our D-Day was stupendous . . . but our new magic formula . . . will be as fabulous as she is.

All these new toys were made possible by plastic fabrication. The themes, the manufacturing, and the materials were all innovative, although the gender division – the doctor set for boys, the nurse set for girls – was strictly traditional. Indeed, the 1949 catalog featured a *Bonnet Box*, which was not only decidedly a girl's toy, but one that reflected Lynn's passion for hats and her background in the fashion industry. Still, even here, there was innovative progress beyond the prewar days, when girls' toys were often about emulating such mundane "women's work" as ironing and laundry. *Lynn's Bonnet Box* was about millinery design and was glamorous and creative.

The *Small Fry Trousseau Trunk*, another Lynn Pressman creation featured in 1949, also spoke to a traditional female aspiration – marriage – but, like the *Bonnet Box*, it was really all about getting creative. It supplied everything girls needed to make hats and dresses, including a bride doll to put them on.

Lynn drew even more directly on her fashion-industry roots with 1949's *Small Fry Magnetic Fashion Show*, which contained a dozen miniature costumes, fitted with metal pieces so that they could be mounted magnetically on the included doll.

Small Fry Bonnet Box

**A Real Hat Box —
Just like Mother's**

The young milliner can start her career with Pressman's Bonnet Box complete with: large doll hats, metal scissors, thread, needle, feathers, veiling, thimble, ribbons,

2218

etc. Hat box has leather handle and is a useful carrying box when young "Small Fry" go on week-end trips. Lithographed in attractive colors, size 10⅝" x 9⅛" x 6".

1 Dozen to carton   Weight 12 lbs.

Suggested retail $2.00
Slightly higher West and South

Small Fry Trousseau Trunk   no. 2206

FEATURES:

Real trunk		Bride doll
Hats to make	Wool and knitting needles	Dresses to sew

A novel idea in a sewing and knitting set. Includes a 7" composition doll, 4 dresses featuring a bridal dress and veil, flowers, 3 hats, ribbons, veiling and feathers for the hat, material for an apron, wool and knitting needles, thread, thimble and scissors. Attractively packaged in a metal hinged trunk box, size 12¼" x 7¾" x 5¾".

1 Dozen to Carton   **Weight 23 lbs.**

28

pressman toy corporation • 1107 broadway • new york, n. y.

everybody | loves | **pressman** | toys & games

pressman toy corporation   1107 broadway,   new york, n. y.

LEFT
The *Bonnet Box* from the 1949 catalog was clearly a Lynn Pressman brainchild.

CENTER
The amazing *Small Fry Trousseau Trunk* in the 1949 catalog.

RIGHT
Pressman's new look, on the 1949 catalog cover.

LEFT
The *Small Fry Animal Yarn Picture Weaving Set*, 1949.

RIGHT
Ring Toss games, such as this example from 1950, sold well for Pressman.

A *Fresher* Logo
and a *Newer* Attitude

The last year in which Pressman issued an all black-and-white catalog was 1947. Two years later, in 1949, the catalog introduced a look that was not only more colorful but at once more playful and more sophisticated, featuring a lighthearted cover illustration that would not have been out of place as a *New Yorker* cartoon. The 1952 catalog included fewer Small Fry products, making way for what the 1953 catalog would deliver.

It was the debut of yet another new logo. While the Small Fry look had been cute, it was cute from an adult perspective. The next new thing was a stick-figure logo that seemed to come directly from a kid's perspective, imagination, and creativity. Fresh, simple, naive, and boldly graphic, it was also strikingly modern and sharply different from anything about the past look of Pressman.

The *new* new logo reflected a newer attitude. It marked the company's advance into a higher-profile commercial echelon. Although it was still decidedly a family business, with husband and wife Jack and Lynn emerging very much as a dynamic duo, Pressman Toy Corporation had also vaulted beyond family status. No longer could it ever be confused with a mom-and-pop shop. World War II had brought a major growth spurt, but the postwar era brought a far more profound change in the public, outward-facing character of the company. It was a leap into the big leagues. Pressman was a toy company that had grown up.

One year before the new logo debuted, the 1952 catalog already set the stage with many new graphic elements. These included the first live models — kids — featured in a Pressman catalog. As the company grew up, so did the Pressman children, including young Jimmy Pressman, who made his own debut in the 1952 catalog as one of those models. Momentous as this may have been in Jimmy's young life, it was an even more significant breakthrough for Pressman Toy Corporation. For the first time, the company's toys were pictured with their ultimate consumers — kids!

In later interviews, Lynn Pressman often spoke about how she had worked to bring the Pressman catalogs to life. As a longtime fashion-industry publicist, she knew that nobody advertised clothing on hangers or even mannequins but on *live* models. Why not do the same for toys? Pressman catalogs were published not for the consumer but for the toy industry — retailers and distributors and buyers and salespeople. Beginning in 1952, the catalogs now reminded everyone in the industry whom they were all really working for. As the kid-centric logo introduced in 1953 implied, everyone was working for the kids.

Small Fry Teacher Set 2232

Featuring Real Slate with "White Blackboard" on Reverse Side

Every piece of classroom equipment needed to set up school right in the playroom is included in this new Small Fry Teaching Set. Set includes:

Natural Slate & White — Pencil
  Blackboard 7" x 11" — Report Card
Plastic Eye Glasses — Attendance Book
Plastic Wrist Watch — Drawing Cards
Chalk — Lettering Cards
Crayons — Wood Pointer
Felt Eraser — Ruler

PLUS REAL GOLD STARS FOR GOOD CONDUCT

Packaged in a stunning Muticolor box with hinged cover, size of box 18" x 11" x 2".

1 Dozen to carton   Weight 34 lbs.

Suggested retail $2.00
Slightly higher West and South

pressman *HAS*

THIS YEAR'S

MOST EXCITING

TOYS & GAMES

...35 sparkling new items at the Fair. Pressman Toy Corporation, 1107 Broadway

Ad leading up to the 1957 Toy Fair.

Chapter 7
Pressman in Print

1949–1957

Under Lynn Pressman's influence, the Pressman ads that appeared in *Playthings*, the leading toy industry publication, became much more theatrical. What were originally straightforward industry-oriented product ads became whimsical, sometimes even teasing, but always with a flair that had Lynn's touch all over them. Pressman catalog covers also became much more exciting, fun, and even provocative.

Pressman industry ads from 1949 to 1952 featured distinctive, sophisticated, and fun cartoons.

Everybody loves Pressman toys and games

Crowds <u>do</u> gather around, *wherever* Pressman toys and games are displayed. They're bright and attractively designed . . . designed to sell. You'll see why when you visit our showroom.

Pressman Toy Corporation, 1107 Broadway, New York 10.

everybody loves **pressman** toys & games

1107 broadway, new york, n. y.

(everybody loves Pressman toys and games)

pressman toy corporation

1107 broadway, new york, n. y.

"D"!

"D-Day" is coming March 9th!

Toy Fair 1953 will see the unveiling of our new **top secret** project (code name "D-Day").

We predict that "D-Day" will be the most revolutionary and successful toy item in 25 years!

"D-Day" is one of more than 40 exciting new Pressman toys and games which will be on display at our spacious new show-rooms at 1107 Broadway. We also promise many interesting improvements in our staple line of over 100 toys and games.

We are now setting up a new factory of over 200,000 square feet which will help us increase our production this year.

Pressman is hot for '53! Be sure to see us **early** on your trip to New York, to assure priority deliveries, or write for 1953 catalogue.

PRESSMAN TOY CORP.
Jack Pressman, President

THIS PAGE
"D-Day" was the Toy Fair launch date for the *Dentist Set* and the new *Doctor* and *Nurse* sets.

OPPOSITE LEFT
Promoting the new *Doctor-Nurse Sets* in the post–Toy Fair issue, March 1955.

OPPOSITE RIGHT
Pressman brings a carnival atmosphere to the 1956 Toy Fair.

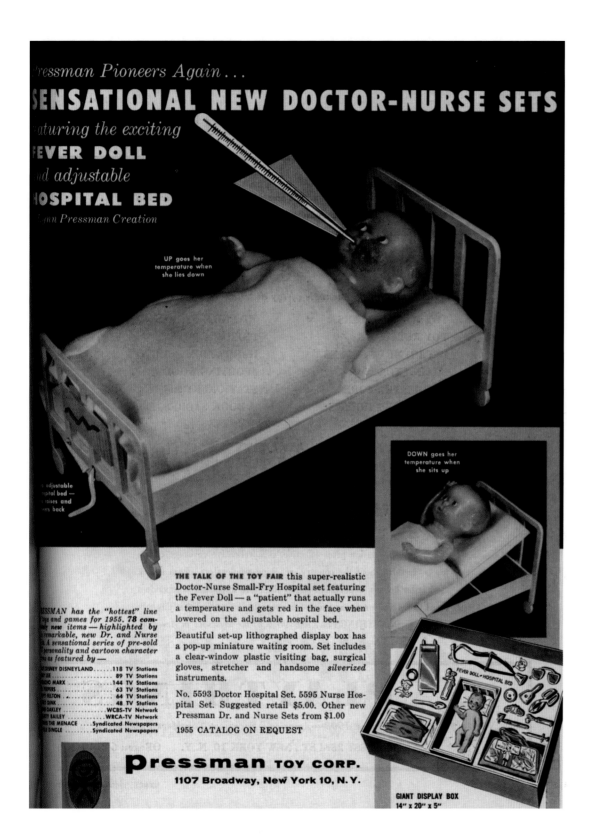

Pressman Pioneers Again...

SENSATIONAL NEW DOCTOR-NURSE SETS

featuring the exciting

FEVER DOLL

and adjustable

HOSPITAL BED

...Lynn Pressman Creation

UP goes her temperature when she lies down

DOWN goes her temperature when she sits up

...adjustable
...pital bed —
...raises and
...ers back

...ESSMAN has the "hottest" line
...ys and games for 1955. **78 com-**
...new items — highlighted by
...emarkable, new Dr. and Nurse
... A sensational series of pre-sold
...ersonality and cartoon character
...as featured by —

...DNEY DISNEYLAND......118 TV Stations
...Y LEE ....89 TV Stations
...CHO MARX ....144 TV Stations
...PERS ....63 TV Stations
...M FELTON ....64 TV Stations
...DINK ....48 TV Stations
...Y OAKLEY ....WCBS-TV Network
...EY BAILEY ....WRCA-TV Network
...IS THE MENACE ....Syndicated Newspapers
...LE DINGLE ....Syndicated Newspapers

THE TALK OF THE TOY FAIR this super-realistic Doctor-Nurse Small-Fry Hospital set featuring the Fever Doll — a "patient" that actually runs a temperature and gets red in the face when lowered on the adjustable hospital bed.

Beautiful set-up lithographed display box has a pop-up miniature waiting room. Set includes a clear-window plastic visiting bag, surgical gloves, stretcher and handsome *silverized* instruments.

No. 5593 Doctor Hospital Set. 5595 Nurse Hospital Set. Suggested retail $5.00. Other new Pressman Dr. and Nurse Sets from $1.00

1955 CATALOG ON REQUEST

Pressman TOY CORP.

1107 Broadway, New York 10, N. Y.

GIANT DISPLAY BOX
14" x 20" x 5"

SUPER-COLOSSAL!
sensationally gigantic!
BIGGER THAN BIG!

Wonder of Wonders!
EXTRA STUPENDOUS

MULTI-GARGANTUAN!
Specially Spectacular!

PRESSMAN CARNIVAL

1956 PRESSMAN TOY CARNIVAL

SIDESHOW *at the* PRESSMAN MIDWAY

REFRESHMENT TENT — serving breakfast, brunch, lunch and afternoon snacks.

SIDE SHOW — Penny Pitch — Dart Games — Carnival Bingo — T.V. — Relaxation for tired Midwayers.

FOUNTAIN OF YOUTH — where foot baths revive sagging arches and heat pads revitalize aching backs.

AND MANY OTHER GREAT ATTRACTIONS!

HURRY, HURRY, HURRY! Step right this way to Pressman... See the toy and game sensations of the year... The F. W.* (the Toy Lady) was inspired by the wonders of the Midway to bring you your biggest sales-builders... Learn all about the great Pressman Toy promotion for '56 that will make extra profits for you... Come one—come all to the Pressman Midway Show Room at 1107 Broadway during Toy Fair... A Gala week of events!

*The Fabulous Wife

pressman TOY CORPORATION

1107 Broadway, New York 10, N. Y.

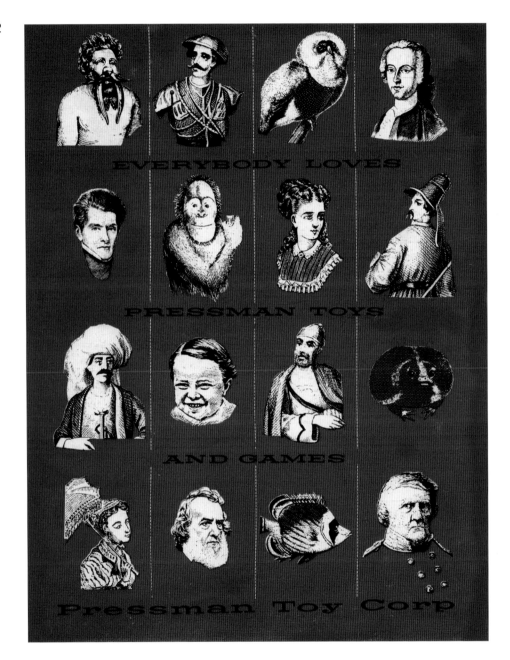

Pressman's distinctive 1951 catalog cover.

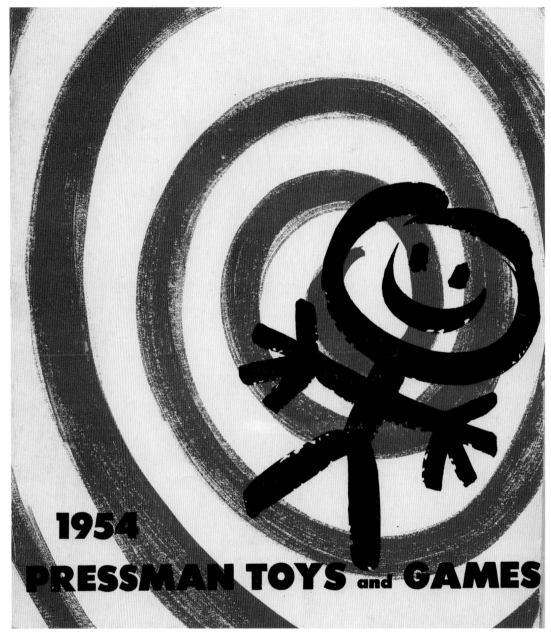

1954 catalog cover.

The thirty-fifth anniversary catalog cover, 1957.

Pressman Toy Corporation at thirty-six.

Pinky Lee Game Time, 1955.

Chapter 8
The Age of Licensing Arrives

1954–1958

"Our creative efforts have developed the finest line of staples on the market, augmented by constant adventures into exciting new specialty items," Jack Pressman proclaimed on page 1 of the 1950 catalog. The company's strategy was clear. While Pressman would continue producing the tried, true, and traditional "staple" toys, there would also be "adventures" into novelty and innovation. Increasingly, beginning in the 1950s, these innovative adventures were tied to licensing. During this decade, licensing from brand-name popular culture evolved from a mere adjunct to Pressman's marketing strategy into a prime mover. And as plastics innovated the material from which the company made its toys, so television, the reach and influence of which grew exponentially during the 1950s, provided the catalyst for innovation in both the theme and content of many of Pressman's highest-profile offerings.

TV's Early Impact

Groucho Marx, who starred with his brothers in a series of classic comic movies, hosted a popular radio quiz show beginning in 1947, which made the transition to television on October 5, 1950. *You Bet Your Life* was an instant hit that was broadcast on NBC TV through 1961. Pressman brought out its *Groucho TV Quiz* in 1954. It included everything needed to play a version of the TV quiz game: questions and answers, Magic Word Cards, and money emblazoned with Groucho's likeness. And the game also furnished the most important things needed to actually *be* Groucho himself: a pair of eyeglasses, a broad mustache, *and* the comedian's ubiquitous stogie.

Although *Groucho TV Quiz* faithfully translated the look of the show to the new product, the game was actually adapted from two existing Pressman games — *Wise Old Owl Geography Quiz* and *Veda the Magic Answer Man*. Both were magnetic toys. *Wise Old Owl* featured a plastic owl figurine, and *Veda the Magic Answer Man* starred Veda, a swami-like figurine. Each held a wire pointer. The player would position the figurine in its base on the game board and rotate it so that the pointer pointed to a question. This action oriented a magnet within the figurine. When the player then put the Owl or Veda on the answer circle, the polarity of the magnet in the base of the figurine relative to that of another magnet mounted under the answer circle magically rotated the figurine's pointer to the correct answer to the question.

For the *Groucho TV Quiz*, the Owl and Veda

Confucius Say was yet another version of the magnetic answer man, 1956.

OPPOSITE
Groucho TV Quiz was an early Pressman TV license in 1954.

"Veda" the Magic Answer Man   no. 2223

Where Is the Country Without Women? Can a Whale Drown? Ask Veda these and hundreds of other interesting questions. Veda is the magic Hindu answer man who spins magnetically, and points the way to knowledge.

Permanent Magnets insure accuracy indefinitely. Each quiz comes with 8 sets of question and answer cards, and additional cards are available separately.

Just place Veda on the Question page, point him at a question and place him on the magic mirror. ZING! VEDA SPINS HIS MYSTERIOUS WAY, AND ALWAYS POINTS TO THE CORRECT ANSWER.

Question cards on History, Science, Music, Sports, Nicknames of Cities plus many other interesting topics come with each game. Comes in 7 color box, size 13¼" x 18¼" x 1½".

2 DOZEN TO CARTON   WEIGHT 30 LBS.

Everybody Loves Pressman Toys

LEFT
Playthings ad for *Confucius Say*, March 1956.

RIGHT
Veda was one of several iterations of the magnetic answer man, introduced in 1951.

OPPOSITE
Pinky Lee Game Time, a 1955 TV license, was packed with masks, cups, spoons, ping-pong balls, miniature bowling pins, paper cups, an egg timer, and more, including "Pin the Tie on Pinky."

were remodeled as a strikingly accurate figurine of Groucho. Two years later, in Pressman's 1956 catalog, *Veda the Magic Answer Man* (in the words of the catalog copy) got "promoted to $2.00 with a brand new face" and was now the focal figure in *Confucius Say*.

Another early example was based on the *Pinky Lee Show*. Born Pincus Leff, Pinky Lee got his start as a vaudeville tap dancer before specializing in slapstick comedy and burlesque-style rapid-fire one-liners. He was a pioneer of early television, with a variety TV series for NBC in 1950 and a fifteen-minute sitcom called *Those Two*. But he became most famous for *The Pinky Lee Show*, a Saturday-morning NBC children's show sponsored by Tootsie Roll, which premiered in January 1954. Each show opened with his theme song, which began, "Yoo hoo, it's me, / My name is Pinky Lee."

Poor Pinky collapsed on camera in 1955 and never appeared again on his own show, which ended on June 9, 1956. But not before Pressman brought out *Pinky Lee Game Time* in 1955.

Pressman began using licensed TV tie-ins to launch and market certain toys. The tie-ins were the company's first promotional use of TV, but it would not be until 1961 — with the debut of a game called *Mastermind* — that Pressman began advertising on television (more on that in chapter 9).

TV tie-ins, beginning with the *Groucho TV Quiz*, were the start of that expansion. TV viewers became loyal to certain shows — the long-lived *You Bet Your Life* among them — and tie-ins sought to transfer some of that loyalty to toys, thereby creating a direct relationship with consumers.

You Bet Your Life was the first game show Pressman licensed, but it was far from the last. The company's three greatest successes in the years that followed all came from adaptations of TV game shows.

**1135 DISNEYLAND
METAL TAPPING SET**

Right Out of Disneyland

Youngsters can create scenes of Disneyland Park
Fantasyland—with all the fabulous Disney cartoon characters – in lovely metal tapping and
engraving, with this Pressman craft set. Includes
14 individual plaques, which may be mounted
on the supply of heavy board backings provided.
A leading *craft* item. Size of box: 14-1/4 x
10-1/4 x 1.

Two dozen to carton   **Weight 35 Lbs.**

Suggested retail $1.00; Slightly higher West and South

© Walt Disney Prod.

1171   DISNEY MODELING CLAY

*Featuring "Scampy"—
New Disney Character*

Something new has been added. Walt
Disney's favorite new character, *Scampy*,
son of Lady and the Tramp, is the new
excitement in Pressman clay sets. Children can model Lady, Tramp and Scampy
with the plastic molds included. Non-
toxic clay in assorted colors in Disney
styled display box. Box size: 15-1/4 x
10 1/4 x 1.

Two dozen to carton   **Weight 45 Lbs.**

Suggested retail $1.00;
Slightly higher West and South

© Walt Disney Prod.

1107 MOUSKATENNIS

Complete Beginner Set

Young children will love these MICKEY MOUSE
shaped paddles with a real net, clamps, and
ball.
Box size: 11" x 8½" x 1½".

Three dozen to carton   **Weight 28 Lbs.**

Suggested retail $1.00; Slightly higher West and South

TOP ROW
More Disney licenses, 1956.

BOTTOM
Mousekatennis, featured in the 1957
catalog, was a child's introduction to
table tennis.

The Disney Licensing Bonanza

The entertainment behemoth now known as the Walt
Disney Company was founded as the Disney Brothers Cartoon Studio in 1923, during the silent film era.
Mickey Mouse debuted in 1928, and, with this iconic
character, Disney and his creations soon became fix-
tures of American popular culture. In December 1937,
the Disney studio's first feature-length cartoon, *Snow
White and the Seven Dwarfs*, premiered. By 1939, it
was the highest-grossing film up to that time, and as
we saw in chapter 3, Pressman eagerly licensed the
Snow White brand for several toys.

In 1955, Walt Disney expanded his entertainment
empire by opening the Disneyland theme park in Ana-
heim, California. That same year, too, his studio's *Lady
and the Tramp* was released, and the Disney presence as a licensing powerhouse became practically
overwhelming.

Pressman's 1956 catalog featured a veritable
galaxy of Disney-licensed toys. Among these was
Walt Disney's Lady and the Tramp Modeling Clay,
which also featured Scampy. Touted as "Walt Disney's
favorite new character," Scampy was the son of Lady
and the Tramp. The set included plastic molds, which
children could use to model Lady, the Tramp, and
Scampy.

The rest of the Disney-licensed line that year related not to Disney films but to Disneyland. These
included *Walt Disney's Disneyland Blackboard*,
which doubled as a desk and featured "exciting
4-color roll top illustrations" depicting "scenes
from Disneyland and many of Disney's favorite
characters." There was also the *Disneyland Metal
Craft Tapping Set*, which gave children everything
they needed to "create scenes of the Disneyland
Park's Fantasyland – with all the fabulous Disney
cartoon characters – in lovely metal tapping and
engraving."

Grouped with the Disneyland-branded toys was
a special version of the long-popular *Duck Pins*,
the *Donald Duck Pins and Bowling Game*, which
captured the "charm of Disney's ever popular
'Donald Duck'" in the graphics on the box and the
game board.

In 1955, *The Mickey Mouse Club* premiered on
television, its original run extending to 1959. The
1957 Pressman catalog offered a wealth of *Mickey
Mouse Club* tie-ins, beginning with *Mousekatennis*, a Mickey Mouse Club–branded incarnation of
table tennis, featuring a pair of colorfully cheerful
Mickey Mouse–shaped paddles.

Other Important Early Licenses

Walt Disney was not the only source of Pressman film, entertainment, and television licenses. The 1956 catalog included a *Dennis the Menace Chalk 'n Slate Set*, which featured the popular comic-strip character created by Hank Ketcham in strips that first appeared in sixteen American newspapers on March 12, 1951. (CBS Television produced a *Dennis the Menace* sitcom starring the child actor Jay North, which was broadcast from 1959 to 1963, but the Pressman toy predated this.)

The same catalog included two different *Annie Oakley Sewing Sets* licensed from an *Annie Oakley* TV series that appeared in syndication and on network broadcast. Produced in 1953, the show was released in 1954, and eighty-one episodes were seen through February 1957.

1172 CHALK 'N SLATE SET

Featuring "Dennis the Menace"

CONTENTS: A large wood framed *real slate*, black on one side for chalk, white on the back for crayons. Also contains box of chalk, box of crayons, felt eraser, stencils, drawing cards and a play clock. Box size: 15-1/4 x 10-1/4 x 1.

Two dozen to carton   **Weight 38 Lbs.**

Suggested retail $1.00;
Slightly higher West and South

1156   ANNIE OAKLEY SEWING KIT

Set features a miniature "Annie Oakley" doll with all necessary material to sew an authentic western costume for the doll. Box size: 14-1/4 x 10-1/4 x 1-3/4.

Two dozen to carton   **Weight 21 Lbs.**

Suggested retail $1.00; Slightly higher West and South

TOP
Dennis the Menace Chalk 'n Slate Set, 1956.

BOTTOM
The *Annie Oakley Sewing Set* from 1956.

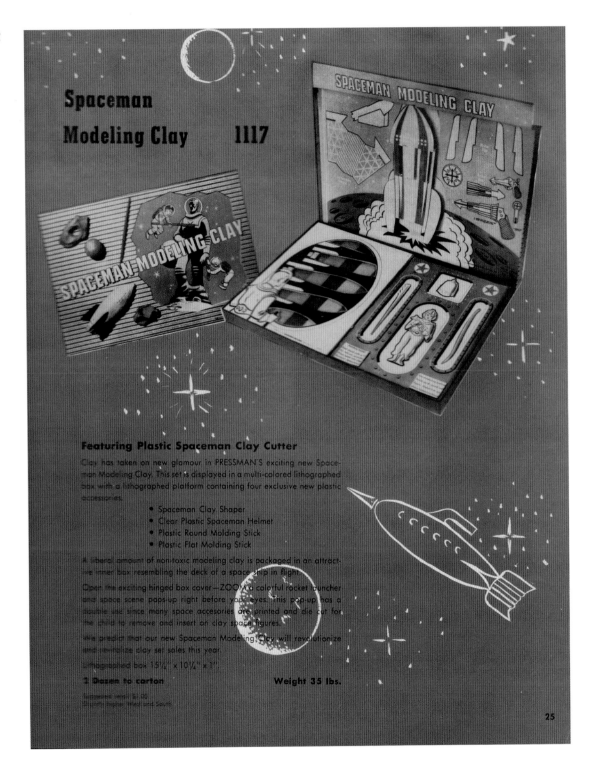

From the Space Age

On October 4, 1957, the Soviet Union launched Sputnik I into low earth orbit — and into global pop culture. The phrase "Space Age" became a universal meme, but Pressman Toy Corporation had beaten the Soviets into the Space Age a full four years earlier. Science fiction, especially featuring space travel, became popular Saturday matinee fare during the early 1950s, well before Sputnik. Pressman was one of the first toymakers to hop aboard this marketing rocket ship.

The 1953 catalog touted a whole fleet of space-themed toys. There was *Spaceman Modeling Clay*, which featured vintage 1950s sci-fi graphics on the box and interior and included "four exclusive new plastic accessories" — a spaceman clay shaper, clear plastic space helmet, plastic round molding stick, and plastic flat molding stick. Space-themed paint sets included two versions of *Pressman Space Paints*, both of which included a "plastic spaceman palette" in addition to paints, crayons, a paintbrush, and mixing tins. The $2.00 set offered more colors than the $1.00 set, and the *Spaceman Paint Palette* was also available separately.

A *Space Captain Magnetic Dart Board* featured on one side a "multicolor space target," with a spaceship, galaxy, moon, Saturn, and other scored objectives. Rather incongruously, a "realistic baseball target game" was on the other side of the dart board.

Perhaps the most interesting Pressman space-themed toy was *Space Faces*. Let's recall Jack's Pledge from the 1950 catalog: to offer "the finest line of staples on the market, augmented by constant adventures into exciting new specialty items." It turns out that, in addition to the staples and the innovations promised in the pledge, a third category had somehow escaped mention. It was the "knockoff" — essentially one company's attempt to replicate the success of another company's toy by offering something similar, though sufficiently different to avoid unpleasant legal consequences.

The *Space Faces* toy is an early example of a quite artful knockoff. It looks like an original, fresh, and playful venture into the realm of good-humored extraterrestrials — straight out of the world of science fiction — yet it is a knockoff of a toy that had been invented in 1949 and was first manufactured by Pressman rival Hasbro in 1952. *Mr. Potato Head* (soon joined by *Mrs. Potato Head*) proved so popular that it is still manufactured today, although the original version, in which plastic facial and other bodily features could be pressed into a user-supplied potato, was replaced in 1964 by a version with a plastic potato.

While the knockoff remains a toy-industry hallmark — a toy-industry "staple," if you will — *Space Faces* managed to give a genuinely new spin on the *Mr. Potato Head* original. This was an achievement rare in a knockoff.

OPPOSITE
Modeling clay goes into orbit, 1953.

RIGHT
Space Faces: a space-age *Mr. Potato Head* knockoff, 1953.

Small Fry Golf
for Boys and Girls

2281

4 Plastic golf clubs in stunning 2 color leatherette golf bag. PRESSMAN brings you a golf set which looks just like "the real thing". The golf clubs have handles the right length for children. The leatherette golf bag has a handy pocket and safe rubber golf ball, individually boxed. Bag is 21" long.

1 Dozen to carton

Weight 15 lbs.

Suggested retail $2.00
Slightly higher West and South

5

Small Fry Fireplace Mantle

3314

Complete with 2 Stockings

What fun for the children to awaken Christmas morning and find that Santa left not only 2 lovely Christmas stockings, but this sturdy fireplace too!

Made of sturdy fibreboard, with lithographed red brick printing and black top and hearth. Complete with Santa andirons. Individually packed K.D.

1 Dozen to carton **Weight 55 lbs.**

Suggested retail $3.00
Slightly higher West and South

61

Live Models!

Thanks to Lynn and her fashion-industry background, the 1950s saw the introduction of live models, genuine kids playing with real Pressman toys. Although various models were hired, the company relied heavily on the two Pressman boys, Ed and his younger brother, Jim. Both later became Pressman Toy executives, and Jim was the company's longest-serving president.

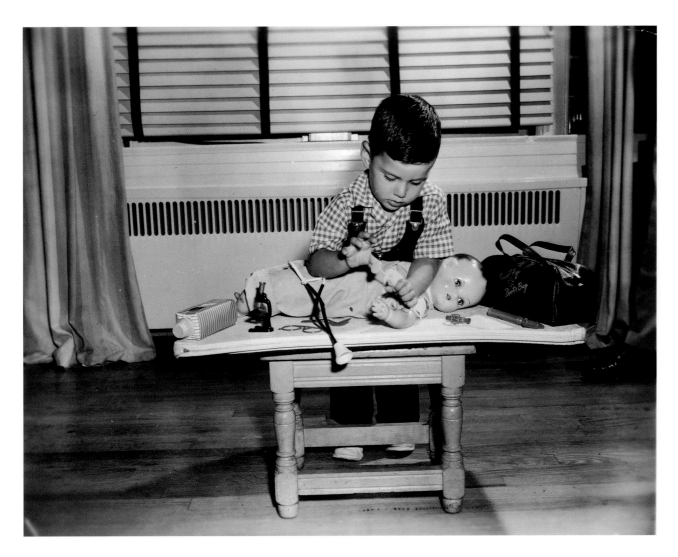

Doctor and Nurse Bags **4494-4496**
Exact Duplicate of the "Black Bag" Doctors and Nurses Carry
Complete with identification tag, costume and telephone

Doctor Bag 4494 An exciting, authentic toy for every little boy. Bag contains a complete costume for child, from full sized doctor's coat and mask to rubber gloves, plus dozens of authentic accessories including plastic telephone and other items pictured (right). Individually boxed, size 11¼" x 5" x 5".

Nurse Bag 4496 Complete costume, from navy cape with red piping and authentic copy of nurse's cap to rubber gloves. Plus all the exciting accessories pictured (right). Same box and size as #4494.

1 Dozen to carton   **Weight 21 lbs.**
Suggested retail $4.00   Slightly higher West and South

Promotional photographs featuring a young Jim Pressman.

OPPOSITE LEFT
Carrying a Small Fry Golf Set in the 1953 catalog.

OPPOSITE RIGHT
With brother Ed in front of the *Small Fry Fireplace Mantle*, 1952.

LEFT
Making use of the *Doctor Bag*.

RIGHT
On the *Doctor and Nurse Bags* catalog page, 1952.

Lynn Steps Up

In popular culture and in toys, the future was a major theme during the 1950s and, for the most part, a hopeful and exciting one. Sadly, however, for Jack Pressman, declining health caused by heart problems was clouding his own future. Lynn became both increasingly devoted to caring for him and to looking after the company he had built and in which she was becoming more and more deeply involved.

As Jack required much time off, Lynn stepped up. By hard necessity, she took up the reins of the company. She had become vice president in 1952 and was elevated to executive vice president in 1956. Members of her family became more visible and prominent in Pressman Toy Corporation. In 1957, Jack's brother Bill, who had been active in Pressman since 1938, left to join major competitor Hasbro. The rift between Bill and Jack lasted for decades. In fact, the brothers never spoke again, and if it had not been for Bill's daughter Penny, who became friends with her aunt Lynn, Bill would never have been heard from again. Fortunately for Jim, Penny arranged for Bill to visit Jim and his wife, Donna, in their New York apartment around the year 1995. This was the first time Jim ever met his uncle Bill, and he was struck by the uncanny resemblance to his father, Jack. Bill later sent Jim the 1916 photograph of the Pressman toy store that appears in chapter 1 of this book along with Bill's handwritten commentary on the picture.

By the late 1950s, Lynn's nephews, Norman and Shelly Oshin and Robert and Herbert Lane, had all joined Pressman as executives. But her impact on the company went far beyond recruiting her kin. Her "woman's touch" extended to the direction of the company's products and presentation. Her imprint is especially evident in the 1958 catalog, which opened with a full-page photo spread of live kid models using the doctor and nurse kits that were products of Lynn's inspiration. The headline on that page proclaims:

PRESSMAN TOY CORP.
STYLE LEADERS IN DOCTOR
AND NURSE KITS

"Style" was what Jack and the others called a "Lynn word." It reflected her fashion-industry background and her approach to marketing both fashion *and* toys. Her aim was to endow Pressman's products and presentation with a stylish look that would set them above and apart from other manufacturers.

Equally telling was what followed the doctor and nurse kits in the 1958 catalog. It was eight pages of sewing and knitting products. Moreover, the "Open Letter to All Our Friends," which was printed on the page facing "Style Leaders in Doctor and Nurse Kits," was signed by Jack Pressman as the company president but was accompanied by Lynn Pressman's name and title, "Exec. Vice President," both appearing just below and to the left of Jack's signature. This was the first time Lynn Pressman appeared in the opening letter.

Jack at the Broadway office playing
Chinese Checkers with sales manager
Dave Uchill, 1958.

Jack's Passing

Jack did preside over Pressman's celebration of its thirty-fifth anniversary early in 1957, at which thirty-five new items were to be debuted at the Toy Fair. "In view of the constantly growing child population, the increasing consumer income figures, and our own promotional plans," Jack proclaimed, "this anniversary year should be our biggest." New vacuum-forming manufacturing equipment had been purchased, and the company's general offices were moved from 1107 Broadway in Manhattan to the factory at 11 43rd Street in Brooklyn, where a "complete IBM system" was installed to "help coordinate production and sales so that the first can quickly and accurately reflect the second in reference to any item on the line," *Playthings* reported in February 1957.

He soldiered on, but he was not getting better. On April 6, 1959, Jack Pressman died at Doctors Hospital, New York City. He was only sixty-four years old and had been leading the company since he founded it in 1922. Heartbroken, Lynn nevertheless took up the mantle and assumed the presidency of the company. In an industry dominated by men, she would meet much resistance. While her inventiveness and imagination, her passion for style, her wit, charm, and sheer energy would make a lasting mark on the company, it was by no means an easy ride for her or for the company. Jack and Lynn had become a team, her improvisatory playful style and marketing flair perfectly complementing his business acumen. With him gone, that hard-edged dimension was wanting and sorely missed.

As for the love story between the couple, the irrepressible Lynn Pressman would go on to remarry twice before she, too, passed away — on July 22, 2009, at the age of ninety-seven. She far outlived Jack Pressman, but it was he who remained her enduring love.

Jack Pressman

JACK PRESSMAN, president of the Pressman Toy Corporation and a man widely known throughout the toy industry, died April 6 at Doctors Hospital, New York City.

Born in New York City in 1900, Mr. Pressman spent his childhood in the Yorkville section of the city. Following his discharge from the Army in World War I, he became a salesman of metal toys for the Gropper Company. Eight months later he decided to go in business for himself.

At about this time the North American Toy Company, a jobbing firm, started to manufacture toys such as zellophones and lead soldiers on a small scale. Mr. Pressman joined the company as a partner, with the firm's name changing to J. Pressman & Company. The line was gradually enlarged to include jump ropes, wood spinning tops and croquet. In line with this expansion the plant was moved from E. 17 Street, New York, to the company's own, larger building at 346 Carroll Street, Brooklyn.

Jack Pressman

In charge of the sales end of the business, Mr. Pressman became acquainted with Chinese Checkers on one of his trips West. He was so impressed with the game's possibilities that he had it put into immediate production to the exclusion of all other items. (Just prior to the Chinese Checker craze which then swept the country, Mr. Pressman had fortunately invested in a marble company, which assured his firm a ready supply of marbles.)

Through subsequent years Mr. Pressman continued to expand the business, searching out new markets here and abroad and building his line to include many basic wood and metal items.

In 1948, six years after his marriage to Lynn Rambach, Mr. Pressman changed the name of his company to the Pressman Toy Corporation and brought Mrs. Pressman, a former stylist, publicity director and buyer for Abraham & Straus and McCreery's, into the business. The firm's successes of the past decade are credited with having stemmed in great part from her contributions in the fields of packaging and toy design.

The obituary in *Playthings*, May 1959.

Pressman Times

A PRESSY TOY

ON TV

COPYRIGHT PRESSMAN TOY CORP. NEW YORK CITY

PACKAGE BY TOY DESIGNERS INSTITUTE

MADE IN THE U.S.A.

ROGER MARIS' ACTION BASEBALL

...story inside

OFFICIAL MA[...]
BASEBALL [...]
ALL META[...]
SCOREB[...]
AUTO[...]
UM[...]

3379 — ROGER MARIS ACTION BASEBALL GAME

Made of all metal and wood construction, the metal playing board is excitingly lithographed in full color with a decorated wood frame. Spring action ball pitcher enables player to actually control each pitch. "Automatic Umpire" bell rings when a strike is pitched. Regular scoreboard for balls and strikes. "Information Sheet" on Roger Maris, also included.

Box Size: 14¾" x 19⅝" x 1"
Packing: 1 dz.
Weight: 33 lbs.
Suggested Retail: $3.00

OFFICIAL R[...]

PRESSY TOY ON TV   OFFICIAL R[...]

A 1963 catalog page for *Roger Maris Action Baseball*, "as seen on T.V."

Chapter 9
A Woman Takes Charge as TV Ads Change the Industry

1959–1963

Each year that followed her 1942 marriage to Jack Pressman saw Lynn's interest in the family business grow, culminating in the 1947 reincorporation of J. Pressman & Co. as Pressman Toy Corporation and the naming of Lynn Pressman as its vice president.

Lynn quickly imported her fashion-industry background not only into Pressman but into the toy industry itself. Never before had toys been thought of in terms of style. They had never before been marketed in ways that created not just a "look" but a *new* look. Jack made it clear to his colleagues, customers, and competitors that he and Lynn were partners in the fullest sense. Ads Pressman published in the trade papers began selling Lynn as much as they sold the latest Pressman toys. Clearly, Jack was keen on building her legitimacy and esteem within the industry. Ads presented her as a creative and promotional asset, even as something of a secret weapon. Moreover, the

CEO backed up his own messaging with a promotion elevating Lynn Pressman to *executive* vice president in 1956.

But there was a limit to what the industry would accept. Lynn was tolerated — even welcomed and appreciated — until Jack's death in April 1959. Then the naysayers began pushing back.

Meeting of committee in charge of upcoming Israel Bonds dinner (l-r): Dave Richman, Jules Kushner, Larry Lipson, David Uchill, Lynn Pressman Gray, co-chairman Seymour Arenstein, Leon Davis, Frank Lynn, Leslie Berger, Merwin Smith, Morris Greenberg

TOP
At this Israel Bond toy industry dinner, Lynn was distinguished by one of her trademark hats and by her gender – the solitary woman among the toy industry titans.

BOTTOM LEFT
Another UJA toy industry dinner where, once again, Lynn is the solitary woman.

BOTTOM RIGHT
Lynn attended this luncheon meeting with her son Ed. Naturally, she was, yet again, the only woman at the table.

At UJA dinner, l-r: speaker Jacques Torczyner, Jacob Brock, Herb Brock, Julius Kushner, (chairman of the toy industry's drive), Lynn Pressman, Nat Greenman, guest of honor Fred Pierce, Phil Cohen, Charles Raizen, David Rosenstein, David Krotman.

Lynn Pressman, President

Lynn's assumption of the reins of power was no accident. The 1956 promotion to executive vice president had deliberately positioned her for succession. But while she was no stranger to the industry, that industry was highly skeptical of *any* woman running a toy company – or, for that matter, any company. The pushback did not come in the form of overtly hostile action but in the strong sense that a lot of men in power were watching and waiting for Lynn to fail.

As the cliché goes, it is lonely at the top. For a woman in charge, the cliché was gospel truth. In 1959, only two other women ran toy companies: Ruth Handler shared leadership of Mattel with her husband, Elliot Handler, who had founded the company in 1945 with Harold "Matt" Matson. Many years earlier, in 1923, Beatrice Alexander, a New Yorker who designed and sewed cloth dolls under the trade name "Madame Alexander," founded the Alexander Doll Company and ran it for the next sixty-five years, selling it in 1988, just two years before she died at the enviable age of ninety-five. That the toy industry had no problem with her is likely due to the fact that they could see nothing wrong with a woman selling dolls – and, at that, specialty "collectible" dolls. Mattel, of course, grew into a major mainstream toymaker, but while Ruth Handler was at the top, she still shared leadership with her husband.

In a real sense, then, Lynn was very much alone within the industry. A group photo from 1959 shows her in attendance at a dinner for the United Jewish Appeal (UJA), a charity enthusiastically supported by many toy industry leaders. Take a look at the image and recall the song that *Sesame Street* made famous: "One of these things is not like the others / One of these things just doesn't belong." In 1959, that picture was worth a thousand words.

In truth, Lynn was an able businessperson. She negotiated with Jack Dorfman of Bankers Trust an urgently needed line of credit by factoring the company's accounts receivable. It was a hard-fought negotiation that won Dorfman's respect and praise. In conversation, he described her as "charming, forceful, demanding, and tough."

But she was not, after all, Wonder Woman.

Clearly, Jack's failing health followed by his untimely death affected her deeply and distracted her attention from the business. The impact of Lynn's leadership on Pressman Toy Corp. would be dramatic, but it was not instantaneous. The 1959 catalog had the very same cover as the 1958 edition, except for the change of year. It was diminished in length and substance, with everything in black and white and the pictures of the merchandise reproduced small and without any sense of design at all. Most telling was the absence of the personal letter from the president, which had become traditional under Jack. The 1959 catalog was the product of a president and a company in mourning.

RIGHT
A catalog cover for a new decade
of Pressman toys.

OPPOSITE
The closing message in the 1960
catalog was the first time Lynn
signed herself as president of
Pressman Toy Corporation.

A New Decade

Lynn could not afford to mourn for long. The pressure was on. Whatever else Pressman Toy now was, it had been *Jack's company*. The founder-president's identity was the company's identity. Legally, Lynn was president. Her task now was to win the personal credibility to go with her title.

The first catalog of the new decade, 1960, ended with a personal letter from the president, Lynn Pressman. "A Message to Our Many Friends" began with the briefest of backward glances, to the founding of the company thirty-eight years earlier, when "Metal toys were few, plastics were unknown, high speed assembly lines were unheard of and packaging and art work were simple and crude."

The rest was a forward-looking message celebrating an industry on the rise, expressing gratitude for "buyers, jobbers, and retailers," and promising continuous progress and innovation. More specifically, the letter drew attention to "thirty outstanding new items" in the current catalog, along with the freshening of "our best-selling items." It closed by stating a vision of Pressman's corporate identity — as "the leader in popular priced toys and games, peg tables, toy chests, with utmost in styling."

Nowhere in the letter is Jack Pressman mentioned, and that final clause — "with utmost in styling" — is all Lynn.

The 1960 catalog was a great start to a new decade, and while Lynn's most immediate priority was keeping the company afloat, she was determined to work toward its re-ascendancy within the industry. She threw herself into leading the company that had been her husband's. Jim recalls dinners around this time when the family went out to a restaurant. Led by Lynn, the conversation was always about the toy company. Jim would ask if the subject could be changed. And it was! For about five minutes. Then it was back to the business.

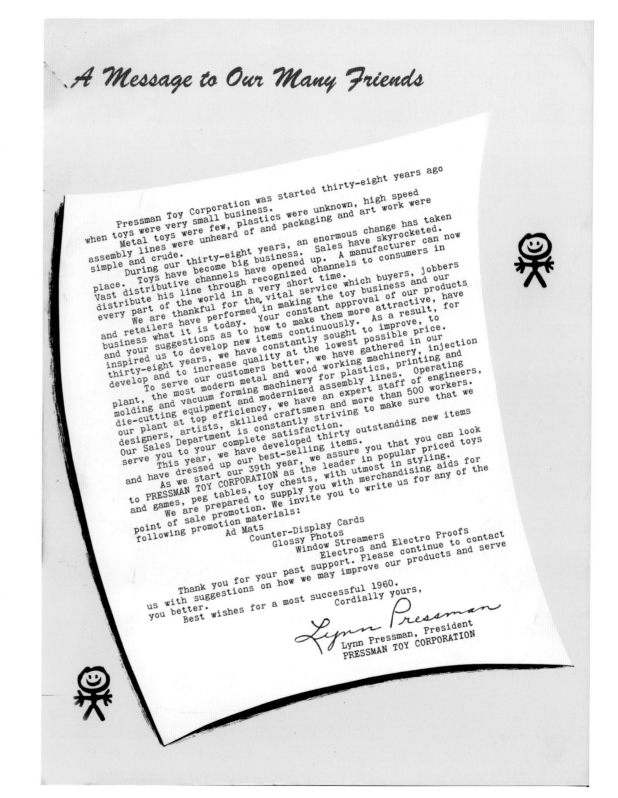

A Message to Our Many Friends

Pressman Toy Corporation was started thirty-eight years ago when toys were very small business. Metal toys were few, plastics were unknown, high speed assembly lines were unheard of and packaging and art work were simple and crude.

During our thirty-eight years, an enormous change has taken place. Toys have become big business. Sales have skyrocketed. Vast distributive channels have opened up. A manufacturer can now distribute his line through recognized channels to consumers in every part of the world in a very short time.

We are thankful for the vital service which buyers, jobbers and retailers have performed in making the toy business and our business what it is today. Your constant approval of our products, and your suggestions as to how to make them more attractive, have inspired us to develop new items continuously. As a result, for thirty-eight years, we have constantly sought to improve, to develop and to increase quality at the lowest possible price.

To serve our customers better, we have gathered in our plant, the most modern metal and wood working machinery, injection molding and vacuum forming machinery for plastics, printing and die-cutting equipment and modernized assembly lines. Operating our plant at top efficiency, we have an expert staff of engineers, designers, artists, skilled craftsmen and more than 500 workers. Our Sales Department is constantly striving to make sure that we serve you to your complete satisfaction.

This year, we have developed thirty outstanding new items and have dressed up our best-selling items.

As we start our 39th year, we assure you that you can look to PRESSMAN TOY CORPORATION as the leader in popular priced toys and games, peg tables, toy chests, with utmost in styling.

We are prepared to supply you with merchandising aids for point of sale promotion. We invite you to write us for any of the following promotion materials:

    Ad Mats
        Counter-Display Cards
           Glossy Photos
              Window Streamers
                Electros and Electro Proofs

Thank you for your past support. Please continue to contact us with suggestions on how we may improve our products and serve you better.

Best wishes for a most successful 1960.

                    Cordially yours,

                    Lynn Pressman
                    Lynn Pressman, President
                    PRESSMAN TOY CORPORATION

DR. BRUNO FURST "NAMES AND FACES"

Game for Teenagers and Adults

DR. BRUNO FURST "THINGS AND PLACES"

A game for the whole family

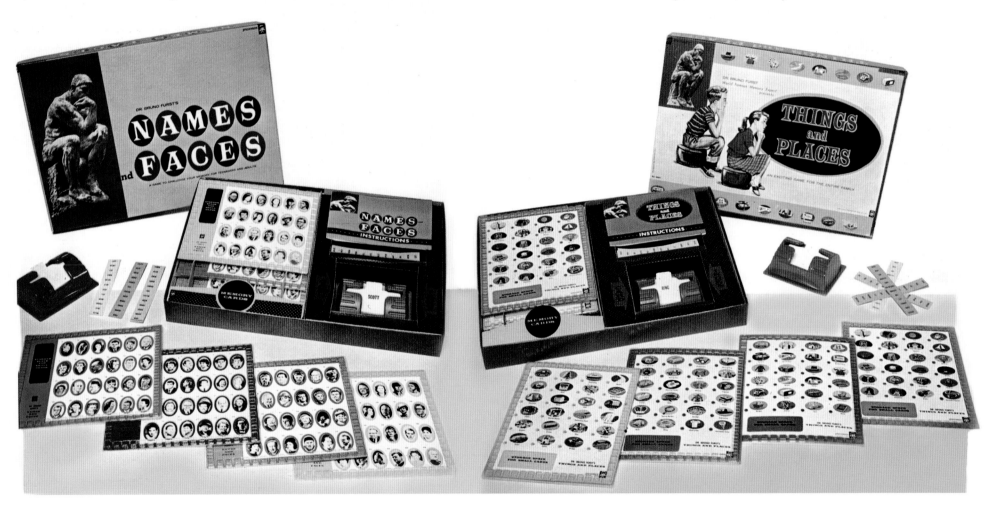

The Dr. Bruno Furst memory games debuted in 1960 on a two-page catalog spread. Furst was "considered the leading memory expert in America."

An Elephant Never Forgets

The 1960 catalog ushered in the decade with four-color printing throughout. The new toys featured bolder and brighter graphics that deserved a full-color presentation. By contrast with even the best of the earlier catalogs, 1960's looked lavish and even glamorous, as did Pressman toy packaging up and down the line.

A line of innovative memory games debuted under the name of Dr. Bruno Furst, "considered the leading memory expert in America today" and described by the *New Yorker* as "perhaps the best all-round mental athlete of the century."

Pressman had licensed movies, Disney characters, and popular television shows to brand any number of toys, but this was something new. It was the use of "expert" branding, which added the imprimatur of a recognized authority to sell genuinely innovative memory games aimed not just at kids but also at "Teenagers and Adults" (*Names and Faces*) and "the whole family" (*Things and Places*).

While these were games and intended to be fun, they also promised to improve the memory of those who played them. This added a compelling dimension of self-help and self-improvement to the games, the debut of which Lynn promoted by bringing a live young elephant to Toy Fair. Before escorting her "guest" to a cocktail party at the Pressman showroom, she paraded the pachyderm outside, at the entrance to the Toy Building, knowing that this was where the press waited to see what new offerings would be coming that fall.

As everyone knows, an "elephant never forgets," but leading in a live specimen suddenly brought a tired memory metaphor to life – spectacularly. It was a publicity stunt with style, flair, and wit. Most important, like the elephant, it was unforgettable.

Young Elephant Lends Weight to Promotion of New Pressman Game

Lynn Pressman helps escort her "guest" to the Pressman showroom.

The Bruno Furst games also foreshadowed a future of innovations aimed at expanding the market for games. There would come a time when Pressman would position itself as a maker of "Games That Bring Families Together."

Lynn launched the Furst memory games with – what else? – a small but very much alive elephant. The verses draped over his back read: "I'm amazed at the way / My memory races / Since I learned how to play / Pressman's Names and Faces."

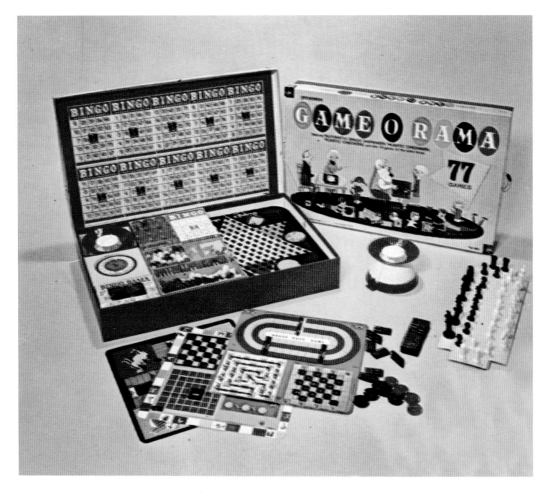

Honoring Jack's Pledge

For all that Lynn did to make her own mark on the company, she continued to honor Jack's Pledge to keep producing a line of strong "staple" items, especially games, as a counterpoint to the continual stream of innovations.

But it was never just a question of producing the tried and the true without also trying something new. Page 13 of the 1960 catalog, for instance, featured three versions of colorful *Game-o-Rama* collections, one boasting seventy-seven "popular" games, one with fifty-eight, and another with fifty-seven – the latter presenting itself as fifty-seven "Games for the Entire Family."

The *Game-o-Rama* sets essentially put old wine in new bottles, creatively packaging traditional and even public-domain games. But Pressman now also sought to innovate such games. A March 1960 trade ad announced, "BINGO . . . but BETTER!" The product was the "new 1960 Monte Carlo Bingo with professional 24″ cage and automatic ball return runway." The promise was "Twice the size . . . twice the value!"

Another innovation was a new emphasis on action games. *Action Baseball* appeared in 1960, a board game featuring a metal playing field framed in wood and with a spring-action pitcher and batter. With plastics no longer a novelty, metal and wood came to symbolize value in "traditional" materials.

The *Action Baseball* idea proved to have legs, and in 1963, *Roger Maris Action Baseball* was introduced as the first of several games licensed by celebrity athletes. Maris, whose MLB career spanned 1957 to 1968, set a single-season record of sixty-one home runs in 1961. It broke Babe Ruth's 1927 record (sixty) and remained unbroken until 1998, when Sammy Sosa hit sixty-six and Mark McGwire seventy.

The doctor and nurse kits, which had been Lynn's early brainchildren, were now well established. In 1960, they received an innovative addition, namely a *Fully Equipped Hospital*. These versions of play-doctor and play-nurse appeared more unisex in content, but they were still marketed as separate doctor (boy) and nurse (girl) playthings.

BINGO . . . but BETTER!

Pressman proudly presents the new
1960 Monte Carlo Bingo with professional
24″ cage and automatic ball return runway.
Twice the size . . . twice the value!

preview at our showrooms . . . now!

pressman
toy corporation
1107 Broadway, New York

108

Extensive 3-Year Expansion Program Begun by Pressman

Lynn Pressman

Stephen Markelson

ABOVE
Playthings covered Pressman's expansion plan in February 1960, including the appointment of Lynn's son-in-law, Stephen Markelson, to the position of vice president and general manager.

OPPOSITE
The visionary *Mastermind* debuted at Toy Fair, 1961.

TV Advertising Changes Everything

In a February 1960 *Playthings* article, Lynn laid out a three-year plan to be executed with her newly hired son-in-law, Stephen Markelson, whom she named vice president and general manager. George Wisun was hired away from Ideal Toy as VP in charge of sales, dedicated to managing sales through chain stores.

These were big moves and big bets on Pressman's future, but perhaps the most consequential component of the expansion was the entry into the high-cost, high-stakes arena of television advertising. In *A Profile of the United States Toy Industry*, Christopher Byrne explains that "no single cultural development transformed the toy industry more than the introduction of television. From accelerating the development of kid culture, unifying children's entertainment experiences nationwide, launching characters, and promoting toys, it was influential on virtually every level."

For Pressman, it was the 1961 debut of a game called *Mastermind* that prompted the leap into that medium. Nothing like *Mastermind* had ever before emerged from Pressman or, for that matter, any other toymaker. Essentially, *Mastermind* was a computer game long before the advent of the PC, Mac, Gameboy, PlayStation, and what have you. Players played against the computer, choosing from games set in outer space and under the sea to simple tic-tac-toe. With a design commissioned from an industrial design firm, *Mastermind* was billed as "smartly contemporary" and priced at an impressive thirteen 1961 dollars.

"Pressman Proudly Presents a TV Spectacular," the 1961 catalog announced. *Mastermind* was so new, so different, that only TV could promote it. But despite national TV advertising, the game was simply too far ahead of its time, and neither the technology of the era nor the game-playing public was quite ready for it. Twenty years later, *MASTERMIND*, a strategy board game, was acquired by Pressman. The name was the same, but there was no other connection with the 1961 game.

PRESSMAN PROUDLY PRESENTS A TV SPECTACULAR

LITTLE BROTHER TO GIANT COMPUTORS THE MASTERMIND'S UNCANNY ELECTRONIC SOUL ALLOWS IT TO PLAY ANY NUMBER OF GAMES WITH YOU — MAKES THE RIGHT MOVES — FLASHES AND BUZZES — CHALLENGES YOU TO BEAT THE MASTERMIND! THAT'S NOT ALL- MASTERMIND IS PRESSMAN'S TELEVISION PERSONALITY, BACKED BY A GIANT TV PROMOTION — MASTERMIND WILL REACH THE HEART OF THE NATION!

1377 THE MASTERMIND Smartly contemporary — styled by HMS Industrial Designers — this fascinating toy acts as an electronic partner in playing outer-space and undersea games — any and all variations of Tic-Tac-Toe.

110

Exciting TV tie-in! Stuff 'n Lace Shari's popular puppets. The lovable Lilliputians of Shari-land now for
the first time made into a cuddly pillow-toy item.

2217   Shari Lewis Assortment   4 ea.   2214   2215   2216

Licensing Triumphs

For Pressman, licensing did not merely grow in the early sixties, it exploded — especially TV tie-ins. Back in 1959, there were the *Huckleberry Hound Press-a-Tile Mosaic Tile Sets*, licensed from Hanna-Barbera's animated TV show and given a full-page *Playthings* ad in April of that year.

In 1961, Pressman released a major TV tie-in with the popular *Shari Lewis Show*, which first appeared on NBC TV from 1960 to 1963. A star ventriloquist, Lewis had puppet friends Lamb Chop, Charlie Horse, and Hush Puppy, each of whom were issued by Press-man as kits to make "Stuff 'n Lace" character pillow toys.

The Adventures of Rocky and Bullwinkle and Friends debuted on network TV in 1959. Pressman's offerings for 1961 featured a *Rocky Crayon Set* while *Bongo Bongo: King Leonardo Game* and *Beany and Cecil* came out a year later.

King Leonardo and His Short Subjects was a TV car-toon series produced by Total Television from 1960 to 1963. Under license, Pressman created an inventive "jigsaw bingo" game that included a bongo drum.

In 1963, Pressman returned to Disney as well with *Mickey Mouse Club* toys, including a *Tell-Time Clock*, a *Spelling and Counting Board*, and a *Counting Jump Rope*.

Pressman even found a way to put its popular nurse and doctor kits together with a toy sensation from Mattel: the Barbie dolls. The 1962 and 1963 catalogs put a licensed *Barbie Nurse* set and a *Young Medic* doctor set on their opening pages.

LEFT
Hanna-Barbera's *Huckleberry Hound* made for a
great Pressman license.

RIGHT
TV's Shari Lewis and her popular hand puppets
translated into appealing Pressman toys.

2208 "KING LEONARDO"
BONGO BONGO
The T.V. program "King Leonardo" features this Bongo Bongo game on their national television spots. It's jig saw bingo. A drum is passed with jig saw parts in it. The child who puts the jig saw together first—beats the drum and is the winner.
Size: 17½"x8¾"x3½"
Weight: 23 lbs.
Packing: 1 dz.
Suggested Retail: $2.00

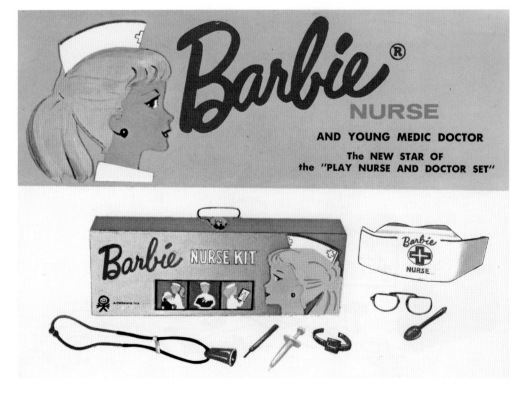

TOP LEFT
The *Counting Jump Rope*, already part of the Pressman line, was given fresh life with a Mickey Mouse license.

TOP RIGHT
A classic TV cartoon show, *King Leonardo and His Short Subjects* was fertile material for a Pressman game – *and* included a "bongo" drum.

BOTTOM RIGHT
Barbie Nurse Kit, 1961, was the first time Pressman licensed a brand from another toymaker.

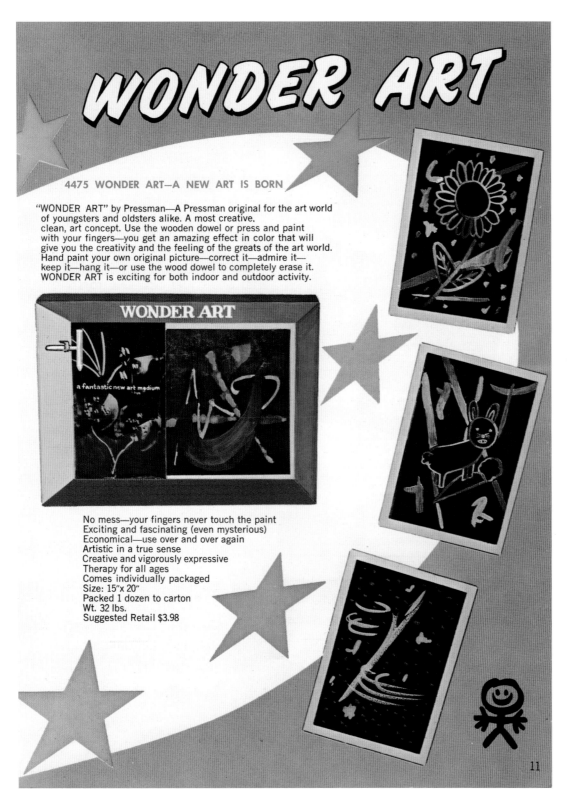

WONDER ART

4475 WONDER ART—A NEW ART IS BORN

"WONDER ART" by Pressman—A Pressman original for the art world
of youngsters and oldsters alike. A most creative,
clean, art concept. Use the wooden dowel or press and paint
with your fingers—you get an amazing effect in color that will
give you the creativity and the feeling of the greats of the art world.
Hand paint your own original picture—correct it—admire it—
keep it—hang it—or use the wood dowel to completely erase it.
WONDER ART is exciting for both indoor and outdoor activity.

WONDER ART

a fantastic new art medium

No mess—your fingers never touch the paint
Exciting and fascinating (even mysterious)
Economical—use over and over again
Artistic in a true sense
Creative and vigorously expressive
Therapy for all ages
Comes individually packaged
Size: 15"x 20"
Packed 1 dozen to carton
Wt. 32 lbs.
Suggested Retail $3.98

11

An enduring success,
Wonder Art was featured
in the 1962 catalog and
in this publicity shot that
same year.

Mrs. Lynn Pressman, Leonard Kushins, and Stephen Markelson.

Wonder Art Merits the Second TV Commercial from Pressman

Page 11 of the 1962 catalog announced, "Wonder
Art—A New Art Is Born." This set enabled "youngsters and oldsters alike" to use their own fingers (or
a supplied wooden dowel) to press and paint colorful artworks without the liquid "mess" of paint. The
following year's catalog devoted a splashy two-page
spread to *Wonder Art*, which became an enduring new
Pressman "staple."

Wonder Art was a Pressman original, which commanded a brand-new vocabulary from catalog
copywriters. It was "exciting and fascinating (even
mysterious)," "artistic in a true sense," "creative and
vigorously expressive." It was even "therapy for all
ages." With *Wonder Art*, Pressman sent toys in new,
creative, even therapeutic directions, and the TV commercial (Pressman's second) promoting it featured
the "acting" debut of young Jimmy Pressman, the
company's future president.

"Let's make paintings the magic *Wonder Art* way!"

"Put away your brushes, your paints, your papers. . . ."

"Make a painting anywhere, without a mess, without a care."

"Get *Wonder Art* today!"

This early Pressman TV ad for *Wonder Art* featured a combination of animation and live action, as well as a catchy jingle. A young Jim Pressman appears bottom right.

114

Lynn Loved Parties

By the close of 1963, Lynn not only had won acceptance in the male-dominated toy industry but had begun to make her mark on it. Part of her success was the product of genuine creativity in toymaking, but part of it, too, was Lynn's charm and flair. The lavish parties she hosted at the annual Toy Fair became legendary, and it didn't hurt that, on each occasion, key buyers "won" artfully rigged prizes.

Lynn made extensive use of her fashion experience. As was the custom in the fashion industry, every year Pressman introduced new styles and new colors. Even more important, Lynn's fashion-industry consciousness enabled her to fully appreciate the promotional power of TV. This medium, she quickly recognized, was quite capable of creating the kind of fads and crazes that would propel the right toys to bestselling status.

In the years that followed those first two television commercials, Pressman used TV to promote whatever they were betting on as their next hot new item. This strategy put the company in the vanguard of a toy industry striving to please buyers and a consumer market increasingly becoming programmed by commercials to look for the hot new craze. Toys and TV came to seem a marriage born in marketing heaven.

TOP LEFT
Lynn with Nat Greenman, founder of a major toy wholesale firm and among the first inductees into the Toy Industry Hall of Fame.

TOP RIGHT
Lynn never hesitated to work her feminine charm on buyers.

BOTTOM
Lynn was known to throw some wild theme parties during Toy Fair.

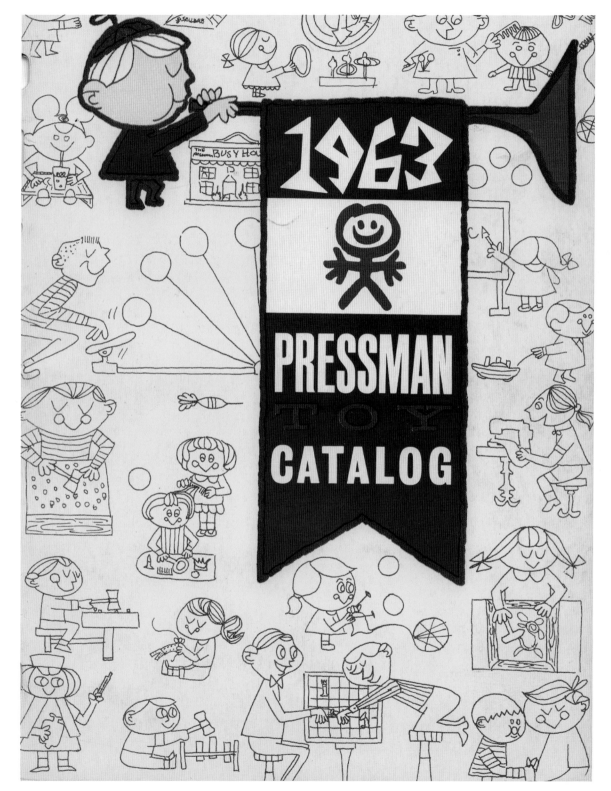

The colorful catalog covers of the early 1960s.

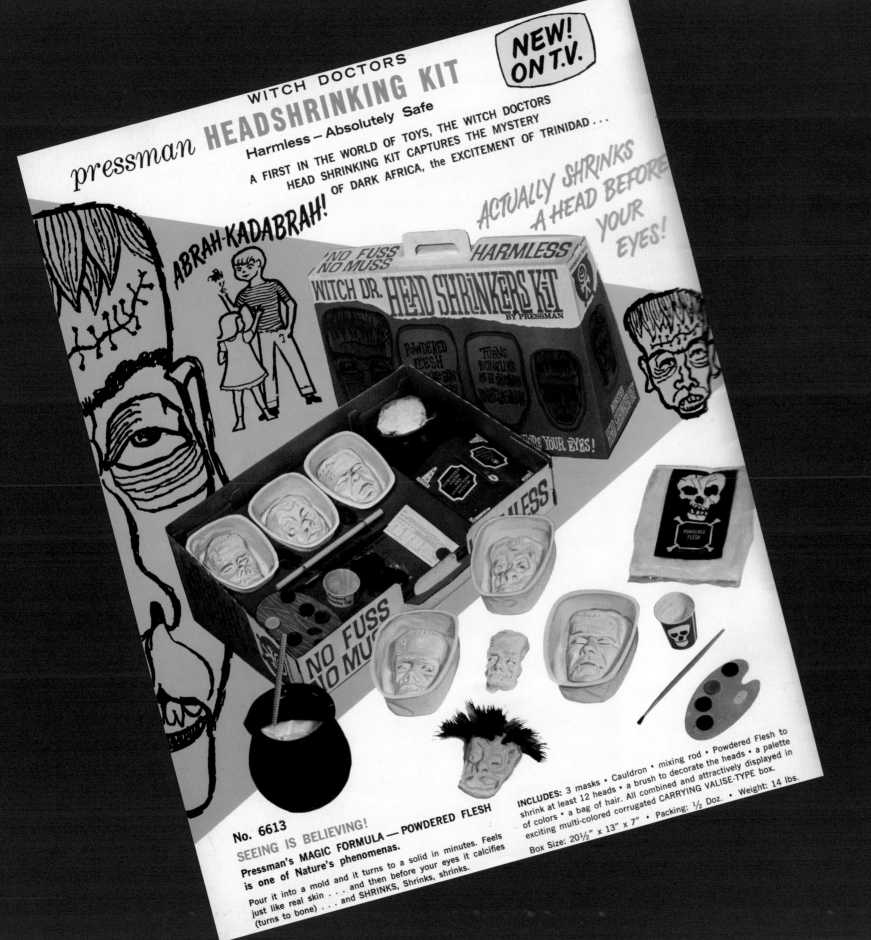

An early use of TV advertising: the 1965 *Witch Doctor's Headshrinking Kit*, complete with "magic formula—powdered flesh."

Chapter 10
Aiming for the Stars
1964–1974

The period from 1964 to 1974 saw many innovations at Pressman, including the meteoric rise of television advertising as well as licensing throughout the line. While Lynn Pressman was in the forefront of many of these new directions, she also continued to honor Jack's Pledge published way back in the 1950 catalog. It was to offer "the finest line of staples on the market, augmented by constant adventures into exciting new specialty items." Whatever innovations emerged between the mid-1960s and mid-1970s, the line was always anchored by a rich assortment of traditional playthings.

A Wonderful World of Color

As plastics revolutionized the toy industry in the years following World War II, so the advancements in color technology revolutionized television. In 1954, NBC made the first regular color broadcast, beaming live the first episode of its new series *The Marriage*. But it was not until the 1960s that color TV sets began selling in large numbers, sales that were jump-started in 1961 by an anthology series on NBC called *Walt Disney's Wonderful World of Color*. Disney's elevation of color prompted more programming, and by the middle of the decade, color shows proliferated. Pressman branded *Wonder Art* with *The Wonderful World of Color* in 1964.

The shift to color television was a major technological development, triggering a significant cultural transformation that was mirrored in the Pressman product line. The 1964 catalog featured the *Invisible Superman Kite*. Here, in one toy, was a spectacular fulfillment of Jack's Pledge. No plaything is more traditional than a kite, but this one was a "Pressman patented development." Nearly six feet tall and four and a half feet wide, it was assembled using "magic clips" rather than the traditional slotted sticks bound with string, and, instead of paper, it was made of rugged plastic, on which a giant Superman was printed. The background was transparent – "invisible" – so that, in flight, the Superman kite really did look like the Man of Steel soaring free.

The kite was a toy designed for mass marketing, and it was pushed with a major television promotion. It paid off, scoring a big hit as what the toy industry called a "counter-seasonal" success. Christmastime is the heyday for toys, but not when you want to catch the winds of March and the breezes of April with a kite. Thanks to television advertising, the Superman kites made for a happy spring at Pressman. It was followed up in a spring and summer catalog with a kite featuring a very different flying superhero: Mighty Mouse.

Another big TV promotion – "New! On T.V." – was 1965's *Witch Doctor's Headshrinking Kit*. Although presented as "Harmless – Absolutely Safe," it did actually shrink "a head before your eyes!" The secret was "Pressman's MAGIC FORMULA – POWDERED FLESH" – "Pour it into a mold and it turns to a solid in minutes. Feels just like real skin . . . and then before your eyes it calcifies (turns to bone) . . . and SHRINKS, Shrinks, shrinks." The TV commercial was elaborately produced, featuring a jungle expedition for the express purpose of finding the secret to shrinking heads.

Television not only acquired color in the 1960s, it became edgier as the 1950s receded further in the rearview mirror. Network TV in the mid-1960s offered hit comic monster series like *The Addams Family* and *The Munsters*, while many local stations across the nation had their own version of *Creature Feature* or *Shock Theater*, which showcased old horror movies.

The *Witch Doctor's Headshrinking Kit* grew out of that media climate, as did a toy called *Luscious Limbs*. Billed as "Another DELICIOUS DETESTABLE toy by Pressman," this provocatively titled item invited children to "Feast on edible ears and other delicious parts of the body." The kit included colorful dry ingredients to be mixed with water and poured into supplied body-part molds. The concoction then solidified into cannibalistic shapes that were actually quite tasty.

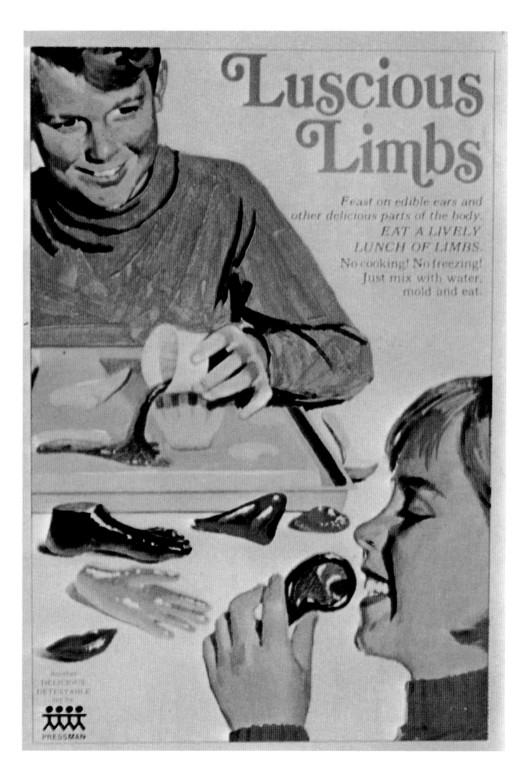

The deliciously detestable *Luscious Limbs* proved that "gross" could actually be quite tasty.

Small World of Dolls
by
WALT DISNEY

PEN PAL DOLLS come with name and address of friend in a foreign land.

POSING DOLLS with bending knees.

CHILE No. 20

SIAMESE No. 10

JAPAN No. 12

SOUTH AMERICA No. 19

SWITZERLAND No. 16

INDIA No. 13

CHILE No. 18

SPAIN No. 15

FRANCE No. 21

AFRICA No. 11

HOLLAND No. 14

SCOTLAND No. 17

No. 1000 CAROUSEL

This charming three dimensional Walt Disney revolving world is made of wood and is beautifully lithographed in incomparable Disney colors. The finished piece is over 24" x 14" high. The revolving world is divided into four sections of the globe, each section representative of a different group of countries. The Small World dolls can be placed into each dimensional scene in different positions . . . and then . . . turn the knob on top and the world will revolve to the lilting strains of the Disney tune, "IT'S A SMALL WORLD." Packed in individual carton, 8 lbs.

SEWING SET No. 4406

SMALL WORLD COSTUME in full color, ready to sew — cut out — match colors and sew. Container is all metal — permanent keepsake of WORLD'S FAIR AND DISNEYLAND. Tray top can serve as "Hostess Tray" or tray for sewing accessories. Contains Disney Small World Doll, fabric for a costume, needles, thread, patterns, scissors.

Size: 9½" Diameter
3½" High
Pack: ½ Doz.
Weight: 20 Lbs.

16

17

It's a Small World

In 1965, Pressman introduced a Disney tie-in intended for girls, *Walt Disney's Small World of Dolls*, which claimed four pages of catalog real estate. The license here supplied a connection not only to Disney but also to the New York World's Fair of 1964–1966, to which Disney contributed "Children of the World" for the UNICEF pavilion. Visitors to the pavilion boarded small boats, which carried them past animatronic sculptures of children in the characteristic dress of various lands and countries. The message was one of global unity – a "small world" – and the exhibit was a hit, inspiring a permanent "It's a Small World" ride at Disneyland. More immediately, it inspired Pressman's *Walt Disney's Small World of Dolls*, with miniature dolls in characteristic dress from such nations as Chile, "Siam," Japan, South America, Switzerland, India, France, Holland, Scotland, and, more generically, "Africa."

Pressman partnered with Lawrence Lipson, chief of sales for the storied Horsman Doll Company, to make the Small World dolls, a move that elevated each doll to near-collectible status. A sewing set allowed children to create their own costumes for the dolls, but the most provocative innovation Pressman introduced came directly from Lynn. Inspired by a letter from the Westchester Women's International League for Peace, she added to the Small World line *Pen Pal Small World Dolls*. Each of these included in their packaging a pen, stationery, information about the doll's country, and the address of a girl in that country. The owner of the doll now had an international pen pal.

OPPOSITE AND RIGHT
Walt Disney's Small World of Dolls was Pressman's take on Disney's *It's a Small World* exhibit at the 1965 New York World's Fair.

WALT DISNEY'S
Small World of Dolls

AMERICA'S TRULY UNDISPUTED MASTER CRAFTSMAN OF CAPTIVATING CHARM, CHARACTER AND COLOR IN HIS CREATIONS . . . WALT DISNEY HAS AWARDED PRESSMAN TOY THE OPPORTUNITY TO BRING TO YOU THE LIVING IMAGE OF ONE OF HIS GREATEST ACCOMPLISHMENTS:

THE DOLL — Walt Disney's "Small World of Dolls" which was exhibited at the Pepsi-Cola Pavilion at the World's Fair 1964-65 — and will be a permanent exhibit in Disneyland in 1966 — was the most popular exhibit at the Fair.

We took a leading SCULPTOR who interpreted the doll into an 8 inch bundle of charm . . . mixed it with a top fashion designer's concept of authentic clothes of many nations . . . merged with a "name" in the doll business who knew all the short-cuts of bringing a quality doll out at a price . . . combined them in our package designers four-color shadow box of Walt Disney Art combined with Pressman's know-how . . . our researchers and merchandisers poured their talents into this captivating lovable doll and when they were finished **we are proud to present**

TRULY AN AWARD WINNING DOLL . . . IN CHARM

COSTUMES — Never did you see such unique charm and originality in design and execution of costumes. The female set will be thrilled with the African costume of pure silk, the toga so accurate in detail, the gold band on the foot, the beaded head band. Each costume lovelier than the next . . . and 48 additional costumes may be had. Each one with accessories. See how children of other lands dress for special holidays, for special festivities, for family occasions and for fun. Dress them . . . undress them . . . love them . . . caress them.

TRULY AN AWARD WINNING DOLL . . . IN COSTUME

PEN PAL — Each doll in the PEN PAL GROUP comes with the name and address of a pen pal in a foreign land . . . supplied to us by the World Ambassadors of Peace, the Caravan of East-West, New York City; fountain pen, stationery, recipes, international dictionary, souvenirs. Embassies of nations cooperated with us for authenticity and accuracy.

TRULY AN AWARD WINNING DOLL IN GOOD WILL AND WORLD FRIENDSHIP

MUSICAL REVOLVING STAGE with Pen Pal Doll. Everyone who hears the "Small World" melody is enchanted with its tune. This tune is captured in the music box which is beneath the stage that revolves our Pen Pal Doll.

CAROUSEL — This revolving world plays the lilting tune of the "Small World." Little girls and big girls can collect these dolls and create their own small world.

TRULY AN AWARD WINNING DOLL . . . IN MUSIC

SMALL WORLD SEWING KIT — Little seamstresses will adore this old time favorite.

TRULY AN AWARD WINNING DOLL . . . IN ORIGINALITY

Dolls Are Ambassadors for Peace

Foreign Costumes Lead Little Girl to Pen Pals

By JOAN COOK

THE time-honored theory has been that little girls played with dolls in preparation for the day when they would be caring for real babies of their own.

Now, thanks to the Westchester Women's International League for Peace and Freedom and a lively brunette toymaker named Lynn Pressman, they may be striking a blow for peace as well.

It all started with the league's antipathy to war and its conviction that toy manufacturers "hold in their hands the capacity for the development of healthy children and mature adults." The group sent letters to New York toy manufacturers in the hope that this might cause them to think and, in so doing, stem the record flood of war toys currently on the market.

The day the letter arrived at the Pressman Toy Corporation was a busy one for Lynn Pressman, as most are since she took over her late husband's business at his death six years ago. As it worked out, she didn't get to her mail until 8 that evening, long after her secretary had left for the day.

Immediate Response

Coming upon the letter from Mrs. Evelyn Straus, president of the organization, Mrs. Pressman responded immediately.

"On impulse, I picked up the phone and called Mrs. Straus and spoke to her as one woman to another. I have a daughter, two sons and two grandchildren and I despise war," Mrs. Pressman explained in a recent interview at her office, 1107 Broadway.

"I told Mrs. Straus that we did not make war toys and that this year we would have in our line a group of 'Pen Pal Dolls,' miniature reproductions of Walt Disney's Small World of Dolls that made such a hit at the World's Fair last summer."

Mrs. Pressman carefully adjusted her Mr. John hat ("I always wear his hats; I have terrible hair"), a froth of printed chiffon draped on a broad-brimmed base, and continued:

"All our dolls have been approved by UNICEF. Each doll comes with a fountain pen, sta-

tionery, menus, recipes and an international dictionary with simple words translated into a variety of languages to enable girls to write to each other with a minimum of help.

"The name and address of a girl in that country are also included."

Authentically Dressed

Pen Pals are supplied by the Caravan, a nonprofit, educational foundation operated by a group of internationally minded Americans. There are currently 20 countries represented by the different dolls, each authentically dressed and many with extra ceremonial robes available where such might be indicated.

Countries include those of Africa, the Far East, France, Russia, Scotland, the Netherlands, the Tyrol, South America, Scandinavia and the Middle East.

One upshot of Mrs. Pressman's person-to-person phone call was a visit from a group of

concerned parents and teachers from Westchester who came to see the dolls and discuss ways in which the growth of toys that dramatize war and killing might be curtailed.

Mrs. Pressman hopes to add dolls from many more countries as time goes on. She tests each new one on her grandchildren, who are delighted to be used as guinea pigs.

Mrs. Pressman can only hope that a new understanding will develop from the contacts the dolls make between girls of different countries. But of one thing she is sure.

"Under no circumstances will I ever knowingly manufacture a bayonet, a hand grenade or any of the other dreadful weapons that can destroy life as playthings for children," she said firmly.

"Pen Pal Dolls" will be available Monday for $3.98 each in the fifth-floor toy department at Macy's.

The New York Times (by Arthur Brower)

Mrs. Lynn Pressman, president of Pressman Toy Corporation, holds one of 20 different "Pen Pal Dolls," all tiny copies of Walt Disney's Small World of Dolls.

LEFT
Lynn appears with comedian Morey Amsterdam in a *Small World of Dolls* publicity photo, 1965.

RIGHT
Lynn appears in a *New York Times* story on the international pen pal feature of the company's *Small World of Dolls* collection, May 8, 1965.

OPPOSITE
Ed Pressman gave the company a new birthday for the 1967 catalog cover. (In fact, the company was "just" forty-five at the time.)

Chasing the Next Hot Item

The toy industry's relentless chase after the next "hot new item" intensified during the mid-1960s. Lynn accorded marketing and advertising a larger role in the business. Her elder son, Ed Pressman, was named director of marketing in 1966 and came aboard with some big ideas, especially related to TV and movies. He later explained that he was determined to "modernize the company's marketing" and make Pressman more "contemporary." Among other things, he brought in Dick Hess, a major advertising art director, to help give Pressman a fresh look.

The TV tie-ins increased in volume and importance. The 1966 catalog featured a whole range of *Batman* products tied into the popular live-action TV show starring Adam West (Batman/Bruce Wayne) and Burt Ward (Robin/Dick Grayson) and based on the DC comic-book characters. There was a selection of *Batman Disguise Kits*, which did not include Batman and Robin disguises but did allow children to be any of three iconic Batman villains: the Joker, Penguin, and Riddler.

In 1967, a black-and-gold catalog cover introduced Pressman:

A Brand New Company • 50 Years Old

The years 1917 and 1967 were prominently featured. It was pure fiction. The historical founding of the company was, of course, 1922, but marketing wanted a golden anniversary, not a sapphire one.

This same year, 1967, Ed employed a hot new ad agency, Adams Dana Silverstein, to promote *Blimps*, which the catalog called "the newest 'hottest' word in the toy industry." The first two principals of the agency were far better known in show business than in advertising. They were Don *Get Smart* Adams

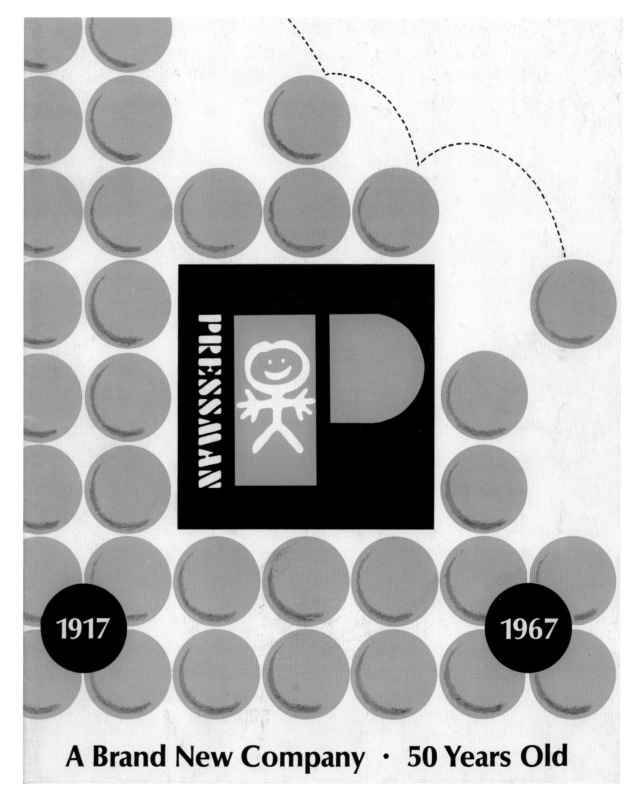

Who Needs Lynn Pressman?

WARD PRESSMAN—DIRECTOR OF MARKETING, PRESSMAN TOY CORP.

Ed Pressman, the company's director of marketing, asks "Who Needs Lynn Pressman?" in a March 1967 *Playthings* ad.

The first thing I did was put her in a jet for Miami. At last... could get some work done.
Eliminating the bugs from our new products and working with our packaging people.
Flying all over for jobber interviews.

Laying out marketing and ad plans with our agency.
Coordinating our million dollar TV-print campaign.
Finally, decorating the showroom for Toy Fair. (Whew!)

Now that we're ready, come on up and see us.
Help us stamp out buttons on our new button-making machine.

Have a piece birthday cake to celebrate our 50th anniversary.
And say hello to Lynn Pressman. She's the one with the great tan.

PRESSMAN
a brand new company—50 years old
1107 Broadway, New York, N.Y.

and comic Bill "José Jiménez" Dana. *Blimps* came in assortments of six or twelve fantastic animals, "flat as pancakes," packed into a colorful cube. "Peel them off, color them with Blimp coloring sticks – blow them up with the magic straw and see them come to life."

Each *Blimp* animal was self-sealing, retaining its shape after being blown up. But each could be deflated and packed back in the cube. The *Blimps* could be reinflated over and over again, and the colors could be wiped off with a dry cloth. The *Blimps* were so unique that, in fact, they received a patent.

Ed Pressman may have been born into a toymaker's family, but he was far more interested in the world of Don Adams, Bill Dana, and their ilk. His first love truly was the movies, and he worked in the family business mainly because he felt he owed the enterprise something for giving him free office space at one end of the Pressman showroom, from which he pursued a career as an independent film producer.

Blimps were heavily advertised on TV in a campaign created by the company's new high-end ad agency, Adams Dana Silverstein, 1967.

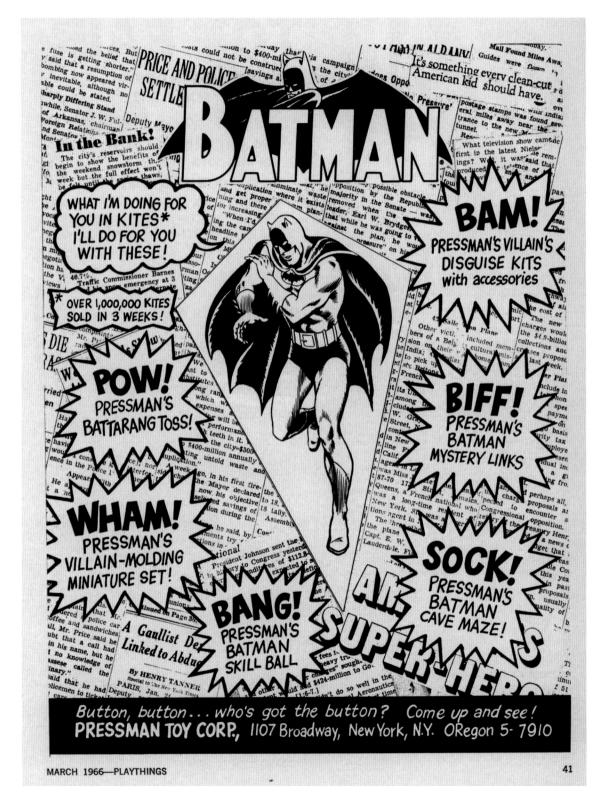

A Pool Boom

Back in its early days, Pressman had cashed in on a miniature golf craze and a fad for table tennis. Throughout the late 1960s, pool tables, scaled down for kids, emerged as an old thing that proved to be a hot new item for the company. It was, for a few years at least, a huge business for Pressman, which made tables in several sizes, with the forty-three-inch most heavily promoted. Pressman engaged in a fierce price competition with another toy company that was into pool tables, Coleco. The resulting price war with Coleco produced big sales but very slim profits.

NEW

LONE RANGER

No. 7750 LONE RANGER WITH HIS HORSE, SILVER

The Lone Ranger is back bigger than ever with a new top rated CBS Sat. TV Show and Pressman has him! A beautiful full color package contains, Lone Ranger with his Horse ready to ride—complete with 40 accessories featuring the world's first *Cold Branding Iron* which allows child to put any of 4 brands on his horse. The Lone Ranger is an injection molded, jointed, movable plastic figure.

Pack: ½ doz.
Weight: 10 lbs.
Box Size: 16¾x14-5/16x4
Carton Size: 16⅞x12⅛x14½"

NEW

TONTO

No. 7751 TONTO & HIS HORSE SCOUT

A beautiful full color package contains, Tonto & his horse, ready to ride. Also 40 accessories including *Cold Branding Iron Kit*. Tonto is an injection molded, jointed, movable plastic figure.

Pack: ½ doz.
Weight: 10 lbs.
Box Size: 16¾x14-5/16x4"
Carton Size: 16⅞x12⅛x14¼"

No. 7752
Lone Ranger and Tonto Assortment

11

Lone Ranger and Silver and *Tonto and Scout*, 1967.

OPPOSITE LEFT
The *Batman Kite* in a *Playthings* ad, March 1966.

OPPOSITE RIGHT
Photo used for the 1966 catalog to promote the new Pressman pool table, featuring Ed Pressman at left.

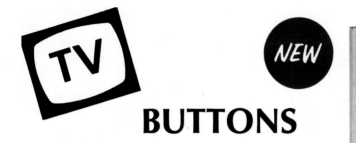

BUTTONS

No. 1869 BUTTON MACHINE

The Mad Fad. Everyone, but everyone wears buttons—campaign buttons, slogan buttons, protest buttons, humor buttons, and here's a real piece of equipment to make them. Made of heavy metal that can turn out "custom" buttons by the thousands. Put a "picture" on, or any "saying". Comes complete with 30 buttons, presstype, pins, and laminating film.

Pack: ⅓ doz.
Weight: 20
Box Size: 21x13¼x5"
Carton Size: 21¼x15¼x13½"

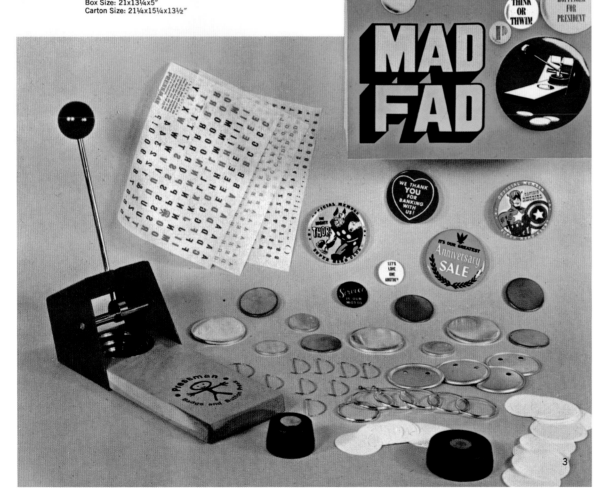

LEFT
The *Mad Fad Button Machine* was promoted on TV in an era when everyone wore slogan buttons.

ABOVE TOP
Demonstrating the *Mad Fad Button Machine* at Toy Fair, 1967.

ABOVE BOTTOM
Photo used for a button featured on the cover of the *Mad Fad Button Machine* packaging. On the far left is Jim Pressman. On the far right is Richard Ablon, one of Jim's oldest and dearest friends.

Try Anything

The claim that 1967 was Pressman's golden anniversary was typical of the "try anything" ethos that pervaded the toy industry in the 1960s. This fabricated bid for more PR was hatched in the incubator of superheated competition among toymakers during an era of saturation TV ads, promotions, and tie-ins. Every manufacturer looked to capture a child's imagination. To some extent, this had always been the goal, but in the sixties everyone fought to reach the kids by dominating the media landscape.

Pressman TV promotions abounded. In 1967, *Blimps* was accompanied by another TV promotion,

for the *Mad Fad Button Machine*, which picked up the decade's passion for pinback buttons. As the catalog copy quite accurately explained: "The Mad Fad. Everyone, but everyone wears buttons — campaign buttons, slogan buttons, protest buttons, humor buttons, and here's a real piece of equipment to make them." The *Mad Fad Button Machine* was made of heavy metal and could "turn out 'custom' buttons by the thousands." It came complete with thirty buttons, press-on type, pins, and laminating film.

Year after year, the pursuit of the hot new item continued as Pressman — and its competitors — labored to create products that promised strong television promotion. Some toys achieved it, but most fell short.

In 1967, successes included the Lone Ranger packaged with his horse, Silver, and another package featuring Tonto and his horse, Scout. Both sets included a number of accessories, including "the world's first *Cold Branding Iron* which allows child to put any of 4 brands on his horse." The toy was licensed from the perennial Saturday-morning children's TV show *The Lone Ranger*.

The popular *Superman Kite* was joined by other superhero kites, including *Batman*, *Captain America*, and, somewhat incongruously, *James Bond 007*, all advertised on television.

Lynn Pressman also looked for other ways to exploit popular culture without directly tying into any specific TV program. In the mid to late 1960s, TV shows of all kinds showed images of hyper-hip young "Mods" wearing the fashion look of London's Carnaby Street. Pressman originated a series of creative kits featuring a cartoon bug named *Connie of Carnaby Street*. She was incarnated in one kit as *The Knitting Bug*, in others as *The Busy Bug* (a combination loom and embroidery set), *The Writing Bug* (which gave kids everything they needed to make their own personal stationery), and *The Glamor Bug* (a jewelry-making set).

ABOVE
Pressman's very busy bug, *Connie of Carnaby Street*, a multiversion Pressman fashion toy from 1967.

LEFT
Lynn's grandchildren, George (*left*) and Jeff Markelson — with buttons.

FISHING GAME

No. 6662 FISHING VIBRO-MATIC ACTION GAME

At last a fishing toy for children that is exciting. A vibrating board makes the fish swim in all directions. 2 to 4 players.

Pack: ½ doz.
Weight: 20 lbs.

Box Size: 18⅛x15⅜x3¼"
Carton Size: 21x18¼x15½"

The Battle for the Basic Game Business

The late 1960s saw the emergence of the latest in a long line of fishing games, this one employing the Vibro-Matic technology that made "the fish swim in all directions." It was an example of a never-ending effort to continually refresh classic games and even the most basic and generic ones, such as checkers, chess, and *Chinese Checkers*. These basic games were a highly competitive space, and Pressman always strove to produce the most attractive versions without pricing them out of reach.

A Changing of the Guard

Ed Pressman moved up to director of marketing in 1967, which became the last year that Lynn's early creations, the doctor and nurse kits, were in the line. "Play Hour" was introduced that year as Pressman's ambitious bid to become a power in preschool and educational toys. The costs of entering this space were high, including the investment in creating injection plastic molds as opposed to the relatively inexpensive tooling required to make many of Pressman's staple games, which were primarily paper based. Moreover, a line of preschool toys needs to be continually updated, whereas the best board games are passed down through generations.

The stick figure logo that debuted in 1953 was revised as a more graphic union of four figures for 1968, and *Tri-Ominos* became a significant nationally advertised "unique twist" on traditional dominoes. In the next decade, the game would break out into a starring role.

The Play Hour line debuted *Crystal Climbers* in 1968, a set of colorful, transparent interlocking shapes – squares, circles, and cylinders – that could be assembled in a free-form manner to reach any height. A European creation, the elegant toy had a contemporary look and invited young children to stretch their imaginations.

During one summer holiday, when Jim was a high school kid, he worked at the Brooklyn factory with classmate and friend Robert Schneider. Their "job" was to create a giant peace sign using *Crystal Climbers*. Jim supposed it had some PR value, with the Vietnam War becoming more and more a contentious issue, but, most likely, it was just something someone at the company dreamed up to keep the boys looking busy.

Hammerons, another building toy in the 1969 Play

LEFT
Tri-Ominos, introduced in 1968, took nearly a decade to become a breakout game for Pressman.

RIGHT
Tri-Ominos publicity shot featuring Lynn with actresses Marlyn Mason (*left*) and Brenda Vaccaro (*right*).

Hour line, promised to satisfy "children's urge to build and create," using sixty colorful plastic pieces, a "wood and metal hammer, box of plated nails and a nailing board." Hammers and nails in the hands of preschoolers. What could possibly go wrong?

The year 1969 also saw company headquarters move to 200 Fifth Avenue, between 23rd and 24th Streets, facing Madison Square Park. Ed Pressman was named president while Lynn continued to serve as chairman of the board.

In 1971, the still-growing Play Hour line debuted the *Play Hour Game*, which was created by Howard

Wexler back when he was working at his first job in the industry at Pressman Toy. Howard became a social worker, schoolteacher, and school psychologist. He earned a PhD in educational psychology from Fordham University and subsequently went into business creating innovative games for children, including (as coinventor) the Milton Bradley *Connect Four* game. By the following year, 1972, Pressman's Play Hour line of toys had reached its pinnacle with the addition of *Pay Phone*, *Flip Form Box*, *Quick Draw*, *Free Form Posts*, *Spelling and Counting Wheel*, and *Thread-A-Block*.

"Play Hour" Pay Phone #6602

Ages: Boys & Girls - 6 months to 6 years
DESIGNED FOR SAFE PLAY

Numbered discs in 3 different sizes and colors are placed into proper slot - guided into dial wheel. Bell rings as discs successfully fall into base container. His powers of observation and discrimination are mastered. Child recognizes likenesses and differences in size and color. Permanent storage area for discs.

PK: 1 Dz. to Ctn. WGT: 27 lbs. BOX SIZE: 12⅝x8-⅞/6x4-7/16 CTN. SIZE: 26⅜x12⅝x17⅝

Play Hour Page 3

Hammerons #2289

Satisfies children's urge to build and create. Easy method to learn coordination. Includes 60 plastic pieces, a wood and metal hammer, box of plated nails and a nailing board 9⅞ x 9, printed in full color.

Hammerons

Give a child a hammer, nails, 60 colorful plastic forms and watch him build a better world on the reuseable composition building board.

BOX SIZE: 11½ X 10½ PK: 1 DZ. WT:

TOP LEFT
Lynn shows her daughter Ann the new Play Hour logo in the new Pressman showroom at 200 Fifth Avenue.

TOP RIGHT
The Play Hour *Pay Phone*, 1972. A cool idea at the time. Less technologically relevant today.

BOTTOM LEFT
Crystal Climbers was the debut item in the Pressman Play Hour line, 1968.

BOTTOM RIGHT
Hammerons invited preschoolers to play with hammer and nails in 1969. What could possibly go wrong?

Game and instructions
created under the supervision of
Oswald Jacoby
world's foremost backgammon authority
and world backgammon champion.

Oswald Jacoby

Backgammon

15" one piece everlast backgammon board with 2 dice, and 30 playing pieces.

PRESSMAN

Upscaling

Ed and Lynn led a movement looking to capture the higher end of the toy market. The Play Hour Boutique was developed as a set of displays for Play Hour toys to be placed mainly in department stores and toy stores. The upscale movement extended to other areas of the company as well. For example, in 1973, Caesar's Series was introduced. Some of the company's traditional games, such as checkers and chess, were redesigned and repackaged with new artwork to make a low-end series look upscale.

But 1973 also ushered in a more imaginative and significant approach to revitalizing at least one traditional game. The company partnered with Oswald Jacoby, a recognized expert on backgammon, to give Pressman's backgammon offerings more than a facelift. Branding versions of the game with a recognized backgammon master gave Pressman the differentiating edge it needed to take advantage of a long-popular but generic game that had suddenly become a craze. Distinguished and professorial in appearance, Jacoby not only wrote instructions for Pressman's backgammon offerings but designed a teaching device called *Auto Backgammon* (featured in the 1974 catalog) and personally promoted the game. Jim Pressman had started working in the company in 1971, and in 1973 he accompanied his mother on a tour with Oswald Jacoby, visiting department stores across the country.

Lynn did not give up on redesigning the look of traditional games. In 1973, she commissioned graphic designer George Gilder to design the Collector's Showcase Series, which featured versions of checkers, chess, backgammon, and go that were billed as "Decorator Games for Display and Play." As the 1973 catalog put it, in these "custom" games, "Elegant crystal clear plastic encases metallic playing boards with

134

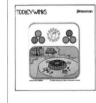

OPPOSITE TOP LEFT
Jim Pressman (*left*) with Oswald Jacoby, a toy buyer, and Lynn, 1973.

OPPOSITE TOP RIGHT
Lynn showing Oswald Jacoby's backgammon book to Jim, 1973.

OPPOSITE BOTTOM
Backgammon was a craze in the mid-1970s, and Pressman engaged Oswald Jacoby, the noted backgammon authority, to issue official rules and strategic advice for play and to become the face of the company's backgammon offerings.

TOP LEFT
The *Parlor Game Series Chess* set came in a box featuring Jim (*left*) playing against designer George Gilder, 1974.

BOTTOM LEFT
Caesar's Series upscaled low-end games with high-end graphics by designer George Gilder.

RIGHT
George Gilder artwork for *African Kala*, a "7000 year old game from Africa," 1973.

Lynn's "LP" logo was inspired by the Louis
Vuitton insignia. Ann Markelson carries an LP
backgammon case as she and brother Jim
Pressman board a plane in this publicity shot.

customized playing pieces." Gilder also redesigned all the basic game packages with highly stylized artwork that provided no sense of what was actually in the box but did give *African Kala*, *Michigan Rummy*, chess and checkers, *Chinese Checkers*, ring toss, and backgammon a new look.

Lynn also worked an "LP" design onto the cases of some toys, emulating the exclusive LV design on Louis Vuitton purses and luggage. She seemed to be trying to present herself as a celebrity face to help carry the brand. The back of the 1973 catalog included "Suggested Ads" for retailers, one of which prominently featured Lynn in a trademark hat.

The upscaling campaign included a proposal to change the name of Pressman Toy Corporation to The Pressman Corporation, with three divisions: Game Division, Play Hour Educational Division, and Adult Game Division. These reflected a plan to continue the expansion of the company in a way that implied a move away from "toys." There would still be games, but the Play Hour playthings for the youngest children would now be branded as "educational," and Pressman would also create a line of games expressly intended for adults. The radical idea of renaming and reorganizing the company came to the verge of fruition in 1974, when Lynn drafted a letter to the industry, but that verge was never actually crossed. Neither the name nor the organization of the company was changed, although another new logo was created and adopted.

A New Vice President

The truth was that Pressman's expansion programs and the relentless pursuit of the next "hot new item" had taken a toll. The company faced formidable competitive challenges, and in this climate, Jim Pressman was named vice president and general manager in 1973.

AT LAST I'VE BECOME A THREAT TO THE TOY BIG SHOTS. NOW, LIKE MARK TWAIN, THEY HAVE ME DEAD. I GUESS BECAUSE I HAVE NEVER BEEN AS SUCCESSFUL AS I WAS THIS YEAR, THEY'RE GETTING WORRIED. DON'T WORRY, THERE'S ROOM ENOUGH FOR ALL OF US AT THE TOP.

SEE YOU AT THE TOY FAIR

LOVE,
LYNN
PRESSMAN

THE PRESSMAN CORP.
200 5th AVE.
N.Y., N.Y. 10010

Lynn's ad in the February 1974 *Playthings*.

Ominos & Strategy Games

Tri-Ominos

Deluxe Tri-Ominos

Travel Tri-Ominos

Tri-Ominos Score Pad

Quad-Ominos
The ultimate domino game

Ages 8 to Adult
For 2-4 players
Convenient storage tray
125 Plastic Tiles

From the makers of Tri-Ominos

Stack Ominos
The three-dimensional domino game.

2-4 players
Ages 8 to Adult

Contents:
56 clear plastic tiles
4 tile racks
1 plastic game tray
1 tile bag
Instructions on back

From the makers of Tri-Ominos

Picture Tri-Ominos
Match pictures and numbers playing the three-sided domino game

Play alone or up to 4 players
35 durable large tiles

Instructions included
Recommended
for ages 4 to 8

The fastest growing family of games of the 70's is soaring into the 80's with our own, special formula for success—now bigger and better than ever!

Each carefully researched introduction of a new game twist expands the loyal and multiplying Ominos market, joined with 12 months of t.v. promotions that capture wide-audience network ratings plus pinpointed local markets—it's an unbeatable combination!

Your profitable Ominos category ... DELUXE TRI-OMINOS (the all-time favorite) ... DELUXE TRI-OMINOS (your solid seller in the higher priced market) ... QUAD-OMINOS (the four-sided challenge for double the fun) ... and STACK OMINOS (the newest sensation in three-dimensional strategy) — now has two sure-to-please additions.

TRAVEL TRI-OMINOS, perfect for the millions who want to take their favorite game everywhere.

PICTURE TRI-OMINOS, the first Ominos to tap the huge young market.

All told, it's a powerhouse lineup that will turn the 80's into THE OMINOS DECADE.

Chapter 11
The Six Million Dollar Man
1975–1980

Jim, the second son of Jack and Lynn, grew up surrounded by the family toy company. He often visited the offices at 1107 Broadway and played on the showroom floor. But, even in childhood, it wasn't a free ride. The 1952 Pressman catalog was the first that featured real live child models using the company's toys. Jim, just turning three years old, was among them. Three years later, he made the cover of the 1955 catalog.

As a teenager, Jim Pressman spent parts of several summers working in the Brooklyn factory. Although his parents had not destined him for an adult career in the family business, and he himself had not planned on such a future, the experience on the factory floor was not forgotten and would prove valuable. After college, Jim did join Pressman Toy and, not too many years after, led the company to its greatest financial successes.

Pressman toys and games 1955

riage of economic stagnation with currency inflation: "stagflation." Against this backdrop, it became clear that the Play Hour line, Pressman's ambitious and costly-to-manufacture entry into preschool and educational toys, had played itself out. Added to this retreat was the cancellation of such off-target product lines as "Banks," "Cottage Craft," and "Plantworld," which littered the 1975 catalog but never shipped a single piece.

Anyone taking a cold hard look at Pressman in the mid-1970s would conclude that the company had lost its direction, and it was in 1975, at the depth of this difficult period, that Jim Pressman was promoted to executive vice president. In fact, only one line of products showed true vibrancy at this time. Pressman's magic shows continued to sell briskly. The truth is that *magic* proved to be the company's lifeline.

Pressman did not simply recycle its many earlier magic shows but introduced a series of sets that all came with an innovative way of creating a stage out of the box using a die-cut piece of printed cardboard. The timing was perfect, because *The Magic Show*, a one-act musical starring Doug Henning, had just opened on Broadway. Magic was having a national resurgence, and the new Pressman offerings were more than an update to a traditional product line. They were an ambitious reimagining of what a kid's magic show should offer. The emphasis was on variety of illusions coupled with genuine showmanship.

In 1983, *The Magic World of Blackstone* would be added to Pressman's magic-show offerings. The son of the legendary Harry Blackstone Sr. (1885–1965), who was known as "The Great Blackstone," Harry Jr. (1934–1997) was a legend in his own right, said to have pulled an estimated eighty thousand rabbits from his hats – or sleeves. He appeared onstage as well as – extensively – on televi-

1975: Jim Pressman Gets a Promotion

President Jimmy Carter famously, or perhaps infamously, labeled the mid-1970s a period of "malaise" for America, as the nation weathered a wicked mar-

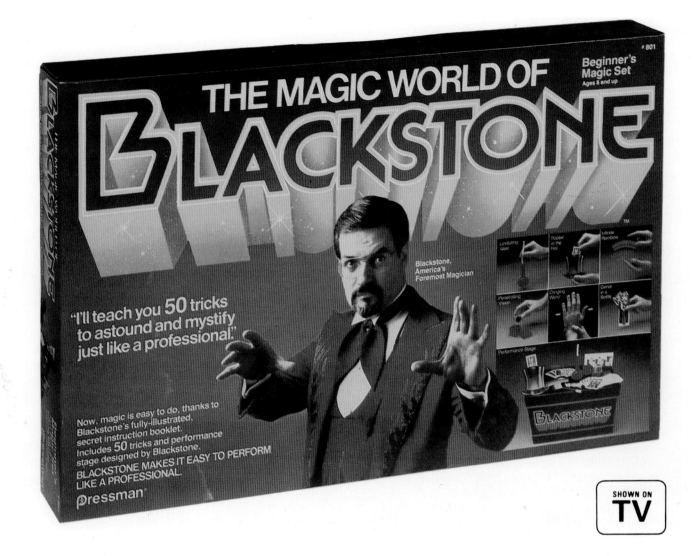

sion, and his magic kits were bestsellers, including the Pressman offering, which promised to "teach you 50 tricks to astound and mystify just like a professional."

While the magic product line prospered, there were other individual toys that stood out in 1975, most notably *Monster Make-Up*. It was promoted as the creation of Dick Smith, a young but already legendary figure celebrated as "the Godfather" of movie makeup. In addition to creating the makeup for *The Godfather* (1972), Smith was responsible for *The Exorcist*, a 1973 supernatural blockbuster that featured the horrific transformation of Linda Blair from a sweet and inno-

cent tween to the head-twisting, pea-soup hurling incarnation of brutal satanic possession. Blair was a fine child actress, but the makeup did the heavy lifting in her role.

The *Monster Make-Up* was not just an effective instance of celebrity/authority branding, it was a genuinely pioneering toy, which was timed to come out close to Halloween before that holiday became big business for toymakers. Subsequently, Dick Smith created a line called *Space Creatures*. It was also during this time that a new movie franchise was being established. It was called *Star Wars*. Any resemblance to creatures from *Star Wars* was purely intentional.

OPPOSITE
Jim Pressman makes the cover of the 1955 catalog.

LEFT
The Magic World of Blackstone in the 1984 catalog.

RIGHT
Harry Blackstone at a Toy Fair event sponsored by Pressman at The Players in Manhattan.

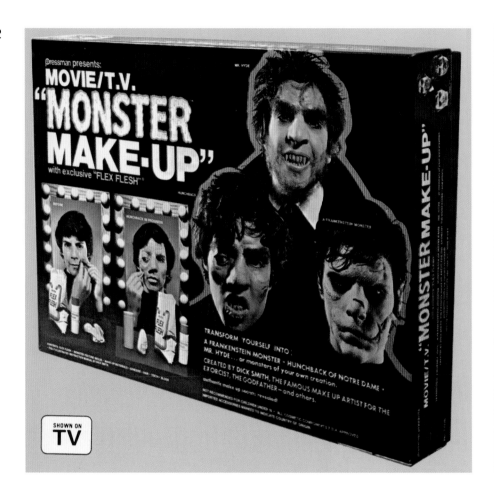

No. 5501 Zordius
Just as lifelike as the others
. . . and sure to make sales
skyrocket!

No. 5502 Megathor
He's got his eyes on the
galaxy — keep your eyes
on the profits.

No. 5503 Vorkan
He looks so real, he could
scare the wearer —
right into your store.

Pressman partnered with celebrated Hollywood
makeup artist Dick Smith to create *Movie/T.V.
Monster Make-Up* (1975) and three super *Space
Creatures* masks (1979).

1976: A New Factory— A New Start

In 1976, Pressman moved its factory from Brooklyn back to New Jersey, this time to New Brunswick. The "new and enlarged . . . modern facilities here," the catalog explained, "will enable us to increase production and improve our delivery and quality controls."

Executive Vice President Jim Pressman took charge of coordinating this major expansion and move, a complex operation that gave his mother, Chairman of the Board Lynn Pressman, the confidence to name him president the following year, after his brother Ed stepped down to focus on his own first love, independent movie producing. Ed did retain the title of "consultant" to Pressman Toy.

The Pressman Toy Corporation has moved to a new and enlarged manufacturing site in New Brunswick, New Jersey. The modern facilities here will enable us to increase production and improve our delivery and quality controls. We thank you, our customers, for making this possible and necessary.

ȹressman

SALES OFFICE: 200 FIFTH AVENUE, NEW YORK, N.Y. 10010 - (212) 675-7910
FACTORY: 745 JOYCE KILMER AVENUE, NEW BRUNSWICK, N.J. 08901 - (201) 545-4000

Jim coordinated the move from this four-story factory at Busch Terminal in Brooklyn to a larger, more efficient single-story building in New Brunswick, New Jersey.

People

Kenner announces appointments to four top executive spots

Kenner has announced promotions of four top executives. David T. Okada, previously senior director of preliminary design, has been named vice president of preliminary design. Okada has been with Kenner since 1973. Louis E. Violett has been named vice president of manufacturing. He previously served as director of production. Violett has been with Kenner since 1974. Armando J. Garcia has been named vice president of international sourcing. He previously served as director of manufacturing engineering. Garcia joined Kenner in 1973. Karl F. Wojahn has been appointed vice president of product integrity.

Barr has named Robert P. Butler director of marketing and sales. Other appointments include R. W. Schaffer, who was named national retail sales manager. Mike Swanbeck was promoted to assistant sales manager and assigned responsibility for sales in the Southeast division. Joanne Hahn was promoted to customer service manager.

James Rambach Pressman has been named president of the Pressman Toy Corporation. Also announced was that Marvin Hellerman, formerly vice president of Ideal Toy, will represent Pressman in the Chain Store Division. Jack Spence Associates will be their representative in the Midwest. J. Dale Everett represents Pressman in the Northeast.

…as appointed Mark D. … engineer in the firm's …elopment department. He …sible for projects in the …nd design of Hedstrom's … and toy wheel goods and …

…**eation** has signed two new …atives for its ABC's Wide …ts, Crown and Cousteau …g goods, family games and …ned were Al Leist & Asso… …gue, Michigan and Barry …ociates of Olympic, …

Mr. Christmas has named Hugh Dryfoos to its staff. Also appointed were four sales organizations to handle the line. Added were Sheldon Company, Pilgrim Sales, McDonald & Associates and Allen Stretfeld Associates.

The Douglas Sales Company, Atlanta, has announced the appointment of Bill Mabry to its sales force. A graduate of the University of Georgia, Mabry will serve as executive salesman with the sales representative firm.

French Toys has appointed Irving Yasny vice president of sales to head up the U.S. sales office for the French-based company. Yasny had been sales director for Matchbox.

Okada Pressman Yasny

Hall-Erickson has appointed Gary D. Showalter to the staff. Showalter's major responsibilities will be with the National Premium Show and the Incentive Travel & Meeting Executives Show. Previously, he was a vice president of Show Company International, and vice president of Far East operations for the Industrial & Scientific Conference Management.

International Playthings, formerly Fischer of America, has appointed Alan Hess national sales manager responsible for the entire sales operation and coordination of IPI's marketing and advertising activities.

Mattel Toys has announced the promotion of Andrew J. McGee to senior vice president, International, Mattel Toys. McGee, who has been vice president, International Operations for Mattel Toys since 1972, will continue to be responsible for all Mattel's International Divisions.

McGee had been vice president and assistant general manager of the International Division of Beech Nut. Earlier associations have included 12 years with General Foods in various managerial positions. Also, he served as associate account executive for Benton & Bowles Advertising.

Mabry Messenger Moss

Eagle Rubber Company has named James A. Messenger national sales manager responsible for directing all sales-related activities in the toy industry, and management of a nationwide network of manufacturer's representatives.

Messenger began with Eagle in 1974 and has held various sales positions including western regional sales manager.

Also appointed was Douglas Kindle to assistant marketing manager responsible for coordinating company advertising, managing marketing research programs and assisting in product development.

Bill Walter and Wally Parsons, both formerly independent toy sales representatives, have joined forces to form a new company, PAW Sales Company, Des Plaines, Illinois. They will cover Illinois, Wisconsin, Minnesota, North Dakota and South Dakota.

North American Recreation Convertibles has named Bravman Associates sales representative for its backyard wood playgound and consumer game tables.

Dale Weller, formerly an independent toy sales representative, has been hired as a salesman by Invicta Plastics USA, Ltd., of New York. Weller will cover Michigan, Ohio, Indiana and western Pennsylvania.

James R. Cavanagh & Associates has been named to represent the Odyssey TV game line made by Magnavox to the toy trade in the Midwest. Magnavox is based in Fort Wayne, Indiana.

SIN, the U.S. Spanish Television Network, has appointed Blank & Kempner exclusive national sales representatives to the toy industry.

92 APRIL 1977 — PLAYTHINGS

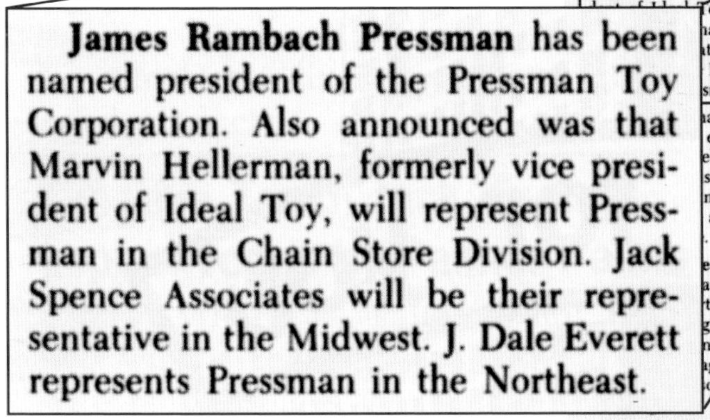

James Rambach Pressman has been named president of the Pressman Toy Corporation. Also announced was that Marvin Hellerman, formerly vice president of Ideal Toy, will represent Pressman in the Chain Store Division. Jack Spence Associates will be their representative in the Midwest. J. Dale Everett represents Pressman in the Northeast.

LEFT
Playthings announced Jim's elevation to company president in its April 1977 issue.

RIGHT
Jim, Lynn, and a buyer.

The New President

Jim had never set his sights on leading Pressman Toy. At Boston University he was an English major. After graduation, he took the summer off and, having no idea what he was going to do for a living, he sought counsel from his older brother. Ed Pressman told him that life was a series of negotiations and, whatever you do in business or in any career, negotiation will be a big part of it. That being the case, Ed reasoned, what better place to learn about negotiation than at the toy company?

It made sense to Jim, who began his career at Pressman in September 1971. His first assignment was to take over what had been a failed effort to market the company's educational toys directly to schools under the banner of Educational Playsystems. This Pressman division had its own catalog, and, in the tradition of the traveling salesman, Jim trekked across the New York area lugging samples in a large metal sample case, visiting Head Start offices and public school district headquarters.

He also promoted Educational Playsystems through mass mailings and telephone cold calls, as well as at

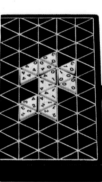

Tri-Ominos Triumphant

the National Association for the Education of Young Children (NAEYC) conference in Kansas City. Some months after this event, he received one of his largest orders, from a parish in Puerto Rico.

It was for $5,000 – huge for a business that typically generated modest orders at best. While Educational Playsystems failed to take off in a major way, Jim, based at the factory in Brooklyn, had plenty of time to learn all about the manufacturing side of the business, from receiving to production to shipping. These lessons stayed with him through nearly a half century at the company.

Promoted to executive vice president in 1975, and with Ed increasingly dedicating his time to Hollywood, Jim found himself well positioned to succeed his brother as president. It was a new era not only for him but for Pressman Toy Corporation. At about this time, Sheldon "Shelly" Greenberg joined the company as its marketing director and was instrumental in guiding Jim Pressman through the momentous decision to refocus the company on just one category of toys: board games.

Jim's promotion to executive vice president had come at a critically challenging period for the company, but his subsequent succession to the presidency took place at an unexpectedly auspicious time.

Tri-Ominos had been introduced years earlier, in 1968, and was briefly advertised on national TV, which helped it to achieve some early success. Soon, however, Pressman turned its attention to developing its new preschool line. The promotion of the game ended, and *Tri-Ominos* was left to fend for itself.

Marketers understand that no form of promotion is more powerful than word of mouth. At the same time, nothing is harder to achieve or more difficult to scale up. Over a long period of benign neglect, however, the word of mouth on *Tri-Ominos* steadily built.

The game, a three-sided variation on traditional dominoes, was doing just fine on its own when, in 1977, Jim and Shelly Greenberg took note of the fact that "just fine" added up to sales of one hundred thousand pieces without any ongoing promotion. Jim and Shelly formulated a strategy refocusing

Tri-Ominos came into its own in the late seventies.

146

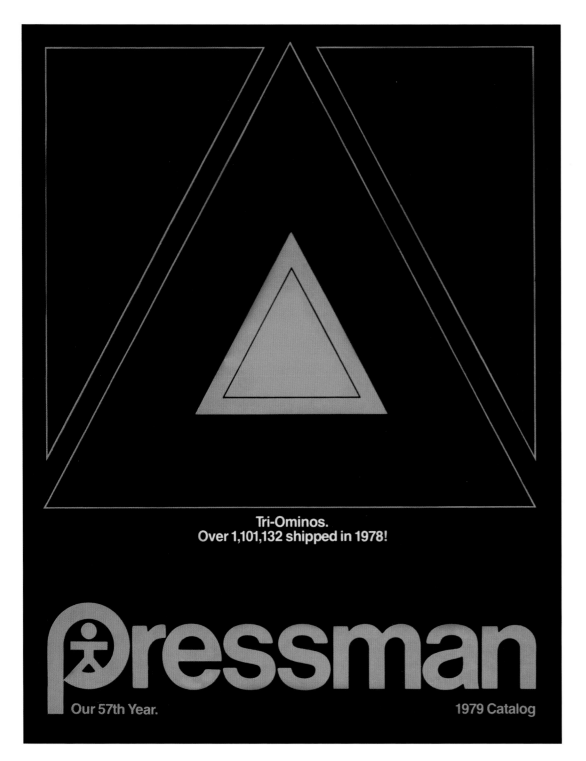

Tri-Ominos.
Over 1,101,132 shipped in 1978!

ρressman

Our 57th Year.   1979 Catalog

Pressman on its board game roots using the newly rediscovered *Tri-Ominos* as its flagship game.

They gave it a brand-new TV commercial, and, driven by national TV promotion, *Tri-Ominos* became an "overnight" industry sensation — eight years after it was introduced. Soon, Pressman launched a deluxe version of the game as well as *Quad-Ominos*, a four-sided variation on the original. It was against the backdrop of this phenomenal success that Jim stepped up to the presidency.

The 1979 catalog cover proudly proclaimed the sales triumph of *Tri-Ominos*, with over one million pieces shipped in 1978. At the 1979 Toy Fair sales meeting, Pressman announced that the company had achieved total sales of over $6 million, a new record.

At this time, *The Six Million Dollar Man* (starring Farrah Fawcett's husband, Lee Majors) was one of the biggest science fiction/adventure franchises going on TV. Ron Gurin, Pressman's vice president of purchasing, called Jim up to the front at the sales meeting and presented him with a *Six Million Dollar Man* action figure. It was a high point for Jim and a historic revenue threshold for the company. Better yet, it was just the beginning.

A Fresh Approach to Marketing

Jim and Shelly made a highly effective marketing team. Their success was driven to an amazing extent by the *Tri-Ominos* juggernaut, which, after two years of TV exposure, was producing half the total sales volume of Pressman Toy.

Yet even as Pressman marketing took on new vigor, the success of *Tri-Ominos* was also directly related to Jack's Pledge from back in the 1950s. It was a promise to continually introduce "novel" toys while also maintaining the line of traditional "staples." *Tri-Ominos* was certainly novel, a genuine innovation, but it was built on one of the oldest and most universal games in the world, dominoes. In effect, it combined within itself innovation and tradition, a combination that has proven exceedingly durable.

Tri-Ominos was also an international licensing success for Pressman. The company eventually licensed it to Goliath for sale in all of Europe. Through this relationship, Goliath became a strong Pressman ally, and the relationship Jim developed with that company led to his selling Pressman to Goliath many years later.

Birth of a Category:
Basic Games

Pressman's decision to focus on board games was part of an effort to sharpen the company's brand identity in an increasingly competitive industry. It was hardly a new identity, board games having been a mainstay of the Pressman brand for most of the company's existence. Pressman expanded over the years from board games into a variety of genres, most boldly making a major investment in preschool products. Now Jim, Shelly, and their team, while continuing to look for innovation and novelty, reversed the expansion. Instead of continuing to dilute the brand, they concentrated it by returning to the company's board game core. This more potent formula would lead to revenue growth, and although *Tri-Ominos* was a spectacular innovation, Pressman created a new traditional product category it called "Basic Games."

Traditional board games possess a perennial popularity. The reason for this is simple. We all grew up playing them. Checkers, backgammon, bingo, *Chinese Checkers* — our parents introduced certain basic games to us, and we, in turn, introduce them to

our children. Traditional board games are therefore perennial sellers. *Everybody*, every parent, grandparent, aunt, and uncle, buys them. A stupendous market is built on this continuity.

What could be wrong with that?

In two words: *public domain*. The basic games are not proprietary, which means that any toymaker can make and sell them. If traditional games are a generic commodity, retailers can buy them from any company, which usually means they typically look for and purchase the cheapest incarnations of each game.

Pressman sought a means of incentivizing retailers to choose its version of checkers, chess, *Chinese Checkers*, bingo, tiddlywinks, and so on over the offerings of a hungry herd of competitors. Across the years, value — the right combination of price and quality — established Pressman's place in the market for traditional games. Well, value was certainly necessary to success, but it was not sufficient to break out Pressman's basic game offerings from the pack.

For a long time, the company had experimented with different distinctive marketing options, especially packaging. Regardless of the design, however, the Pressman game box always used illustrations to depict the game inside — that is, until, under Lynn Pressman, sophisticated abstract artwork was introduced. It was distinctive and attractive, certainly, but it did not offer a visual clue to what game was inside the box.

In 1979, Pressman made a daring move to create a strongly branded line of Basic Games by packaging each game with the *same* bold and distinctive design. Within the company, these basic games were known as the "Red Line," because of the prominent use of bold lettering against a red background on the boxes.

Each box featured a large photograph of the game inside, and the graphic design of the boxes was commandingly bold yet uniform. The games were intended to be displayed together in the store, arrayed on an aisle endcap, which is the

The 1979 catalog cover celebrated the triumph of *Tri-Ominos*.

Year 'Round Favorites

In just a few short years, Pressman's by-now famous "red box" line of popular games has become recognized as the industry leader in quality components, packaging impact and value pricing. To our already comprehensive line, we've added two new dominoes families and an impressive cribbage category — making Pressman the only source you'll need for a complete, year 'round game profit center.

most coveted real estate in a department store, big-box store, or large toy store. The idea was to make a single overwhelming impression on the shopper. The look of the massed Basic Games boxes was dynamic, commanding attention in store aisles, even from a distance.

Instead of marketing individual games, Pressman began selling the whole line and making that line stand out from the offerings of others. It was a marketing strategy inspired in part by the emergence during the 1970s of so-called private label products in grocery stores. These "store brands" were identified as high-value items, combining low price with reliable quality.

Before Pressman launched the Basic Games concept with its distinctive packaging, games were distributed throughout the catalog and even distributed widely across retailers' shelves. In effect, each game was marketed and merchandised as a stand-alone item. The new approach was to market them as a complete line. This would appeal both to retailers and to shoppers, who knew they were getting a high-quality game at a great price. Moreover, the shopper in search of checkers was drawn to a display of the entire Red Line and ended up checking out with checkers, chess, and, on a good day, bingo, too.

This retailing strategy worked remarkably well. While Pressman had always been a player in the "basic game" category, the company suddenly shot up to become one of the leaders in the industry. What is more, the success of this Red Line endures some forty years later, virtually unchanged.

The year 1978 was critical to growth for Jim Pressman. He had decided that it was time for him to hit the road and take over leadership of the sales force. This gave Jim the opportunity to meet the key customers at their offices. The knowledge that he gained by being on the front lines was invaluable. He listened to the buyers, understood their needs, and created programs on the spot.

In those days, New England was the home of many large retail chains – Child World, Hills, Bradlees, and KB, to name a few. Dave Feldman had been with the company since 1956, first traveling throughout the South and Southwest. "Traveling" meant driving, lots of driving, but Dave was tireless and as dedicated and loyal a salesperson as has ever lived. By the late 1970s, he was responsible for New England. So, when Jim became the de facto sales manager, he got into Dave's car and headed north. The trip after Toy Fair was always the key trip of the year. That's when you solidified everything that was discussed at the Fair.

Dave and Jim had an unbelievably successful trip. But that's not how it started. The buyer at Bradlees said he was going to drop Pressman Toy as a vendor. The year had not been a good one for Bradlees.

At the time, the Pressman line was transitioning from Play Hour Preschool to focus on games. But transitions don't happen in just one year. So Jim took a breath and started to pitch the "new" Pressman – the company with *Tri-Ominos* and a new line of Basic Games. By the end of the visit, the Bradlees buyer kept Pressman as a supplier and purchased a few key games.

Nice save. But the highlight of the trip came at Hills, where the buyer said he wanted to knock out their current supplier of basic games and carry Pressman's entire range of red-box Basic Games! With that, Dave and Jim drove back home. It felt like they were flying. And by the end of that fateful year, sales reached six million dollars.

It was just the beginning.

Basic Games – often called the "Red Line" because of their arresting red packaging.

The *Rummikub* Story

By 1979, Pressman had built a strong reputation as a significant player in the game segment of the toy industry. The company's national distribution with America's retailers had grown by this time to include every major chain. This new status attracted the attention of an executive at Toys"R"Us, then the largest toy retailer in the world, prompting him to suggest Pressman as a possible landing spot for an Israeli-invented game called *Rummikub*.

Rummikub synthesizes elements of the card game gin rummy and the tile game mahjong, using 106 numbered tiles that include two jokers. Players are dealt fourteen tiles at the outset of the game, and they take turns putting down tiles from their racks into sets called "groups" or "runs." At least three tiles are required to make a group or a run, and players unable to play from the tiles in their hand draw a tile. The first player to use all their tiles racks up a positive score based on the total of the other players' remaining hands.

The Israeli family who invented the game made several attempts to gain US distribution, but toy buyers were not interested in making a deal with a foreign toymaker having but a single product to offer. Micha Hertzano, son of the game's inventor, Ephraim Hertzano, ran the business in the United States, but he knew that prospects were limited without a larger partner to achieve mass distribution.

In 1977, the original insult comic, Don Rickles, appeared on *The Johnny Carson Show* and raved about how his wife loved playing this game called *Rummikub*. Suddenly, Americans were shopping for *Rummikub* – which was almost nowhere to be found. The Hertzanos were thrilled but realized that they could not meet the new demand because they were manufacturing in Israel. Moreover, their costs – and therefore their asking price – were too high for many consumers. Worse, while they spun their wheels, South Korean manufacturers began churning out cheapo knockoffs.

Rummikub became a key addition to the Pressman game line. *Deluxe Rummikub* was the original Israeli set. *The Original Rummikub* was Pressman's popularly priced version.

Micha Hertzano redoubled his efforts to secure an American partner and soon found himself in a meeting with Jim and Shelly in Pressman's New Brunswick factory office. Jim was aware of the success of the game and its knockoffs and so, following a remarkably brief negotiation, *Rummikub* became part of the Pressman line.

From the beginning, the chemistry between the two enterprises jelled. The Hertzanos ran a small family toy company, and although Pressman had grown, it was still very much a family company, too.

At the time that Pressman concluded the deal with the Hertzanos, *Rummikub* had already developed a small but strong following in places like New York, Los Angeles, and Florida, all of which had large Jewish populations. Often, the game was brought back from a trip to Israel or presented as a gift by an Israeli who was visiting relatives or friends in the States.

To grow these seeds into an orchard, Jim and Shelly decided that they needed a major push to rapidly gain wider popularity. Appreciating that the initial American demand for *Rummikub* had come courtesy of TV's *Johnny Carson Show*, Pressman made its first *Rummikub* TV spot in 1982. The company also diversified the line by bringing out a popularly priced set, which was the lead item, as well as a travel version and a deluxe version. The combination of media promotion, high-volume domestic manufacturing, variety in versions, and popular prices, as well as Pressman's standing in the market, made *Rummikub* a mass-market success.

Pressman's Got the Games

Tri-Ominos, the Basic Games line, and *Rummikub* heralded a major new chapter for the company, which was summed up in a headline in the 1981 catalog: "Pressman's Got the Games."

Chapter 12
Pressman's Got the Games
1981–1984

The toy industry possesses a unique genius for creating national, even global, cultural crazes. No other industry comes close. Think *Silly Putty* and *Hula Hoops* in the 1950s, *Trolls* and *Etch-a-Sketch* in the 1960s, *Star Wars* action figures in the 1970s, and *Cabbage Patch Kids* in the 1980s. Every toymaker hopes to trigger a stampede that lasts a long, long time.

Board Game Game Changer:
Trivia Adventure

The board game sector of the toy industry has also produced its share of craze-making. In the 1930s, it was *Monopoly*. In the 1980s – *Trivial Pursuit*. Both games have had long, long legs.

Trivial Pursuit was created in 1979 by a pair of Canadian newspapermen who, while fighting a hot bout of *Scrabble*, were suddenly inspired to invent a game of their own. Two years later, in 1981, *Trivial Pursuit* was released in Canada, where it was an instant sensation. It was licensed by a US game maker that same year, and it took the nation by storm.

By 1984, *Trivial Pursuit* was generating nearly $800 million in sales, having spawned a subindustry of specialized spinoffs from the original. It was in that year that Pressman introduced *Trivia Adventure* and immediately found itself swept up in a board game craze of its own.

Trivial Pursuit was conceived by adults as an adult game. "Trivia," after all, is the kind of miscellaneous knowledge that accretes, like barnacles, after years of exposure to the world. A pair of young adults, Mary DiMauro and Philomena Chiapetta, both twenty-one-year-old Canadian schoolteachers, had a brainstorm: Why not create a form of *Trivial Pursuit* especially for children? They took their concept to Steve Morris, sales manager of the Canadian toy company Playtoy, who gobbled up the bait. With DiMauro and Chiapetta, he developed *Trivia Adventure*, which the company manufactured and distributed in Canada.

Playtoy had a long relationship with Pressman, dating back to the presidency of Lynn Pressman, when Playtoy was still run by its original owner, Moe Smith. By the early 1980s, Moe's son Jerry was in charge, and it was he who struck a deal with Jim Pressman authorizing Pressman Toy to manufacture and distribute *Trivia Adventure* in the United States.

By 1984, "trivia" was rapidly becoming a crowded board game category with numerous companies scrambling to usher their offerings into the arena. There were, for instance, trivia games based on the gossipy TV news magazine *Entertainment Tonight – ET*, for short – which had debuted in 1981, and *People* magazine, by 1984 in its tenth year as a circulation juggernaut. Another successful knockoff was based on *Ripley's Believe It or Not*, a pop culture evergreen that launched as a bizarre-facts newspaper cartoon feature in 1918 and by the 1980s was a franchise that included a TV show and a chain of for-profit museums.

Amid this broad backdrop of competing spinoffs and knockoffs, *Trivia Adventure* shot to number two in sales, behind only the original *Trivial Pursuit* itself. In fact, *Trivia Adventure* catapulted Pressman to an entirely new position in the game sector of the toy industry, claiming for the company the top spot in the children's game category. This translated into a high-octane boost for Pressman sales, which shot to over $20 million for the first time in the company's history.

What is more, the success stuck. And Pressman Toy never looked back.

MASTERMIND—A Big Deal

Trivia Adventure was a breakthrough success, but it was not Pressman's first major board game triumph of the decade. Two years earlier, in 1982, Pressman Toy had made what was – and remains – its biggest single deal when the company purchased the US rights to *MASTERMIND* for $3 million.

Recall from chapter 9 that, back in 1961, Pressman had produced a game called *Mastermind*. Only the first letter of the name of that game was capitalized, whereas every letter received the uppercase treatment in the 1982 game. But that was far from the only difference between the two. The 1961 *Mastermind* was, for all intents and purposes, a "desktop" computer game some twenty years before IBM marketed its PC, the first practical desktop computer. Far in advance of the necessary technology, it was little wonder that *Mastermind* was less than a success.

Other than the name, the 1982 *MASTERMIND* had nothing in common with the earlier product. *MASTERMIND* was a board game, not a computer, and its point of origin was a company called Invicta Plastics, a UK corporation that was neither a game maker nor a toymaker. It was a small specialty plastics company that made certain point-of-sale accessories for British pubs and had a small side business making school supplies. A subset of its school supply line was a

modest catalog of plastic educational toys, including toy scales and math blocks.

But one product stood out from these classroom-oriented learning games. *MASTERMIND*, as Invicta's box copy explained, was a two-player code-breaking game that taught "cunning and logic."

Invicta released *MASTERMIND* in 1971, and it eventually became the bestselling game in all the UK, winning the coveted title of Game of the Year for the UK in 1973 and Game of the Year for Europe in 1975. Invicta USA and *MASTERMIND* enjoyed huge success in the States as well, and for a couple of years, *MASTERMIND* was even the bestselling game in the USA. But, by 1981, the American company and its British parent fell on hard times, having overproduced many unsuccessful spinoffs of the game, including a failed electronic version. To bail itself out, Invicta needed to sell what had become its main asset: none other than *MASTERMIND* itself.

For Pressman Toy, this was a rare opportunity to purchase a game that was already a modern classic. The acquisition of *MASTERMIND* gave Pressman a solid roster of strategy games, alongside *Tri-Ominos* and *Rummikub*, so that, two years later, in 1984, when *Trivia Adventure* was released, that breakthrough game joined what was already a formidable lineup.

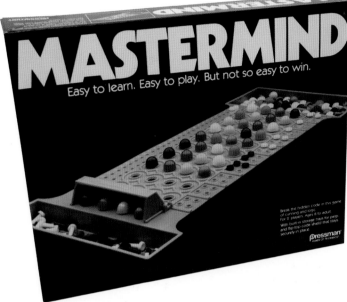

Easy to learn. Easy to play. But not so easy to win.

Another Bull's-Eye

As Pressman's reputation and position within the game sector of the toy industry rose during the first half of the 1980s, a merchandise manager for Target Stores, Marsha Hanson, came to Jim Pressman with a big idea.

The Target chain, which opened its first store in Roseville, Minnesota, in 1962, had by the 1980s evolved into a fresh new concept in large discount stores. At the time, Walmart and Kmart were national giants, the competitors to beat. Instead of confronting them on their own turf, however, Target designed its own unique appeal. It did not emulate the bargain basement look of Kmart or the warehouse look of Walmart. Instead, Target created a new discount merchandising model with brightly lit stores that were stylishly designed shopping spaces, offering customers a more sophisticated, more upscale line of merchandise than its major competitors stocked. The price points were often higher but still better than those of department stores, and the shopping experience was more appealing. Instead of being a last resort for people who could not afford department-store prices – or who lived far from those mostly metropolitan stores – Target styled itself as a shopping destination of choice, which nevertheless offered value pricing.

Marsha Hanson's notion was to bring this upscale discount style to the kind of basic games Pressman Toy was already well known for. She wanted to offer Target shoppers quality checkers, chess, and dominoes at prices that were modestly higher than those of generic no-name versions of these games but still represented an excellent value. She was confident that the Target merchandising model had already accustomed a large cadre of customers to paying a little more than they would at the bargain basement

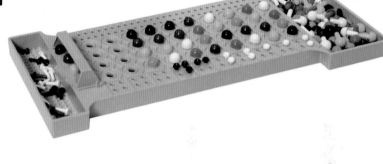

and warehouse retailers in return for a more attractive product of obviously higher quality. And while the customer got a better game, Target reaped more revenue and better profit margins from its higher price points.

At the time Marsha approached Jim, Target was already a regular Pressman customer, and Marsha and Jim had developed an effective working rapport. She saw Pressman as the logical, obvious choice for a company that could create a special line of basic games that, in the initial year of their release, 1983, would be sold exclusively in Target stores. Beginning the following year, 1984, what was now called the "Tournament Line" appeared in the Pressman catalog and was made generally available to retailers.

The Tournament edition of dominoes became a huge seller, as did chess. Players of both games enjoyed the look and feel of quality, and Pressman replaced cheap wooden dominoes with pieces molded of urea, a plastic material that is both durable and beautiful. Also available was a chess set with "hand-carved Staunton wood chessmen" featuring felt bases. Instead of folding paper game boards, the chess sets included an inlaid board that formed the top of a wooden carrying case built to store

THIS PAGE AND OPPOSITE
MASTERMIND – all capital letters – was a major acquisition in 1982.

LEFT
Tri-Ominos meets *Rummikub* meets *MASTERMIND* on the 1982 catalog cover. Pressman's "core games" are established.

RIGHT
Catalog cover from 1983.

OPPOSITE
The Tournament Line of games was originally created for Target Stores.

the chessmen elegantly. *Tournament Backgammon* included a "ready to go padded leather-look carrying case," which opened out to a woven cloth playing field with "sewn-on pips." As for dominoes, the Tournament edition featured a nice wooden storage case, and the urea dominoes had "brass studs for ease in mixing."

In addition to the quality of the games themselves, the packaging included elegant photographic "portraits" of the games inside. As the 1984 catalog explained, the Tournament Line was an entry into the "game market for the 'dedicated game player.'" The new line was presented as the product of "much research," which enabled Pressman to enter "this marketplace having the advantage of being better than the competition."

The Tournament Line set a new standard for everyone, and, with it, Pressman emerged as the industry leader in games, not just in terms of sales but also in quality and appeal. Pressman was now positioned to redefine the market for board games during the second half of the 1980s. The Tournament Line changed the very nature of the "basic game" business. No longer was the trade in traditional public domain games the bottom rung of the toy and game industry. It was now a branded, high-quality, high-value competitive space.

Breaking Out

Pressman had lifted itself out of the well-worn grooves that had long been established for games. The hard and fast notion that there were children's games and there were adult games and the twain could never meet no longer ruled Pressman. From now on, the company would begin creating what it headlined as "Games people play. Together." With this, the emphasis turned to the family and other forms of play that bring people together for fun and challenge.

Tournament Line

The game market for the "dedicated game player" has remained viable and constant throughout the years. Now, Pressman is proud to introduce a complete line of high quality favorites. After much research, Pressman enters this marketplace having the advantage of being better than the competition. Just compare — the difference is obvious! This exclusive line is also available on L/C which will, of course, create higher profits for you!

Chapter 13
Games People Play.
Together.

1985–1991

Since the 1920s, Pressman's steady growth had been fueled by a core of reliably profitable toys and games. What was about to happen in the second half of the 1980s was totally unpredictable. To this point in its history, the company had never had the bestselling game in the country, but that changed in 1985 when Pressman Toy licensed the home version of the TV game show *Wheel of Fortune*.

162

TOP
Jim presents Merv Griffin
with the one-millionth
Wheel of Fortune game
produced.

BOTTOM
The first megahit game
show Pressman licensed,
Wheel of Fortune proved
a long-lived success for
the company.

Spinning Fortune's Wheel

Created by longtime talk- and game-show host turned media mogul Merv Griffin, *Wheel of Fortune* became a juggernaut that continues to be popular today. A slow start, when it arrived on NBC daytime in 1975, gave little hint of the future phenomenon. In fact, *Wheel* largely failed to gain traction when it started in syndication in September 1983 and was carried in only nine markets. The largest of these was Philadelphia, but network affiliates in the biggest markets, such as Chicago, Los Angeles, and New York, showed no interest.

However, with Pat Sajak as host and Vanna White as the letter-turning hostess, things started to change rapidly. By the start of 1984, *Wheel of Fortune* was reaching 99 percent of all US households and was on track to become the highest-rated syndicated program in television history. At its peak, forty million viewers watched *Wheel* five times a week.

The spin of fortune's wheel put Jim Pressman in Philadelphia when the game show was in its early days there. He was in town visiting one of his company's important retail buyers, who suggested he take a look at *Wheel of Fortune*, which was having huge local ratings, even though no one was talking much about it nationally.

Sniffing the possibility of a show on the verge of breaking through, Jim tuned in and was sold. He quickly negotiated licensing rights with Griffin's production company, King World. The paperwork completed, Pressman Toy began creating a home version of the game, the company's in-house designer, Bruce White-hill, developing a unique concept of how to play it at home. It included a plastic game board to display the word puzzle; a reusable card, complete with wipe-off crayon, to record used letters; a spinner standing in for the wheel, and, of course, play money, plenty of play money.

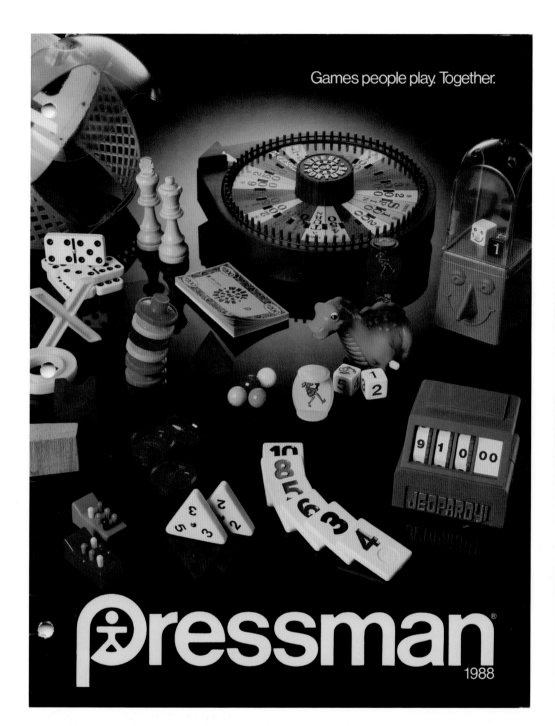

LEFT
The 1988 catalog cover introduced the tagline "Games people play. Together."

RIGHT
A wealth of games, old and new, for 1989.

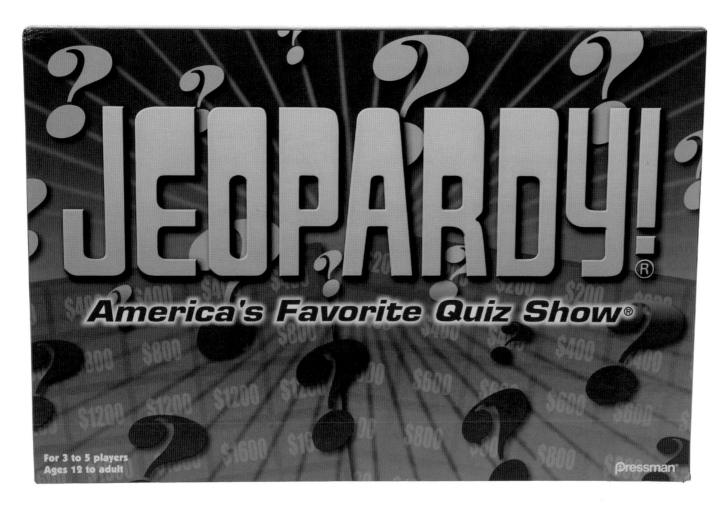

Doubling Down on *Double Dare*

Wheel of Fortune was spectacularly successful, but just as important, it paved the way for Pressman's even greater successes, all based on TV game shows. In fact, during Jim Pressman's tenure as president, the company licensed more than a dozen games from TV game shows.

In 1986, Pressman Toy introduced another Merv Griffin creation, a home version of *Jeopardy!* The catalog for that year announced, "One of the most successful game shows of all time is now a brand new board game!" This was no exaggeration, as few TV game shows have enjoyed the longevity and loyal following of *Jeopardy!* As it turned out, however, while the Pressman game proved to be a solid seller, it ran a distant second behind *Wheel of Fortune.*

Then came yet another leap into promising though unknown territory. In 1986, Nickelodeon, the child-friendly cable network, was a new venture trying to find its audience. It had had a hit show or two, but the operation was still very much a toddler. In October 1986, the network debuted *Double Dare.* A game show in which two teams competed to win money and prizes by correctly answering trivia questions and completing various stunts called "physical challenges," it reminded Jim of a TV game show he had watched as a kid. *Beat the Clock* originally ran from 1950 to 1961, pitting contestants against one another – and the clock – in a competition to complete stunt-like "challenges" before time ran out.

As Jim saw it, *Double Dare* was *Beat the Clock* for kids. In this incarnation, it was a fresh and original variation of a proven winner, and he immediately wanted to license it. While translucent green slime – soon to be a trademark feature of much Nickelodeon programming – could not very well be translated to a home version, Jim was confident that his company

Announced in the 1985 catalog, the game sold 1,250,000 units in 1985, generating $14 million in sales. By 1986, Pressman shipped two million units of the standard game, which was enough to make *Wheel of Fortune* the number one game in the country.

But wait! There's more!

The company shipped almost a million additional units of a deluxe version of the game and four hundred thousand of a "junior" version. The Pressman factory was put on three shifts to turn out *Wheels* twenty-four hours, six to seven days a week, just to keep up with demand. Sales for the company soared to over $50 million, and Jim traveled to Atlantic City to personally present Merv Griffin with the one-millionth game off the assembly line.

could make the game work. He soon discovered, however, that finding an alternative to slime was not the only obstacle that had to be overcome. Reaching out to Nickelodeon, he found that the network had no licensing department. Undaunted, he went directly to network president Geraldine Laybourne, and, after a series of presentations and negotiations, he secured the rights to the game. In fact, Pressman Toy became one of Nickelodeon's very first licensees.

Soon after Jim licensed *Double Dare* but before the game began shipping, the show broke out. It expanded from exclusive cable distribution to syndication for on-air broadcast. Suddenly, *Double Dare* would be seen not only by cable subscribers – still a limited viewer segment in the 1980s – but by anyone, anywhere with a television. In a meeting at a licensing show just after the syndication deal had been made, Geraldine Laybourne told Jim he had "really stepped into a gold mine."

It certainly seemed so. The game Pressman created was highly imaginative and compulsively playable. "First – you're asked a question," the 1988 catalog explained. "Will you answer – or take the PHYSICAL CHALLENGE?" Players who chose the challenge would get to use "the incredible Double Dare stunt system . . . a unique design that lets you plug in props and wear them on your head, waist, arms and legs" while the relentless "timer keeps ticking."

It was a really, really *good* game, and that was important, of course, but it was the synergy with a hit cable/broadcast TV show that launched *Double Dare* to the next level and beyond. Pressman sold over two million games – in the first year alone. This instantly made it even bigger than *Wheel of Fortune*. What is more, the company sold the game at a higher retail price than *Wheel*. The astounding result was that sales reached $67 million in 1988. The following year, sales continued an amazing climb to over $80 million. Once again, Pressman just barely made the game fast enough to satisfy demand as it shot to the status of industry bestseller.

Pressman Toys releases new Double Dare game at American Int'l Toy Fair

Rich and Famous

In 1988, Pressman ventured outside of the game-show genre with another major television license, this time (as the 1988 catalog announced) "inspired by the hit TV show, LIFESTYLES OF THE RICH AND FAMOUS," hosted by over-the-top English entertainment reporter turned TV host Robin Leach.

The late 1980s glorified conspicuous consumption — "Greed is good," corporate raider Gordon Gecko proclaimed in Oliver Stone's 1987 *Wall Street* — and Pressman created a game perfectly echoing the *Lifestyles* ethos. Players guessed the price tags of items and adventures in "six tantalizing categories: 'Champagne Wishes and Caviar Dreams,' 'Posh Playthings,' 'Glory Days,' 'World's Best,' 'Runaway with the Rich and Famous,' and 'Tycoons & Big Money.'" The winner? Why, the one who finishes the game with the most money, of course!

Pressman's *Lifestyles of the Rich and Famous* was a prelude to the next decade of licensing, which included not only TV shows but movies, books, and even popular toys — from other companies!

LEFT
Launching *Double Dare*. *Left to right*: Michele DiLorenzo, Nickelodeon; Sam Goldberg, Pressman; Gerry Laybourne, Nickelodeon; and Jim Pressman, Pressman.

TOP RIGHT
Marc Summers, original host of *Double Dare*, and Jim Pressman kiss Donna Pressman in this publicity shot for the game.

BOTTOM RIGHT
It's thumbs-up for *Double Dare*.

Getting into the Action

Wheel of Fortune and *Double Dare* were high points of Pressman's game-show games. During this period, however, the company also developed some of its most successful action games.

An action game had to entice players to do more than use their minds and move a checker, chessman, or other game piece. Since the core of an action game was — *duh* — action, the game maker had to figure out a way to advertise and promote action. This was difficult to do in the pages of a catalog or in the print of a magazine or newspaper ad.

No. *Action* games cried out for a medium that loves *action*, and no modern medium loves it more than television.

When Pressman got into action games, it went all in on high-priced television commercials designed to grab young audiences and motivate them to ask Mom and Dad to buy this or that must-have game. Given the high cost of TV, action games were a high-risk, high-reward enterprise. Not only were the ads costly, but, typically, the design, tooling, and materials required to manufacture the *action* in an action game required a substantially greater investment than the typical board game.

And there was one additional risk: success itself.

Because great ads mean nothing if a company fails to produce sufficient inventory to support the demand they generate, Pressman always had to build up ambitious levels of inventory in the hope and expectation that a good TV campaign would create high demand. This was wonderful — provided that the demand materialized. If it did not, the company could find itself stuck with an unwanted surplus of expensive inventory.

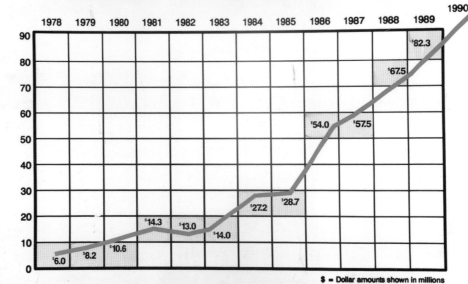

TOP
Jim with Robin Leach, host of *Lifestyles of the Rich and Famous*.

BOTTOM
The chart Jim Pressman showed at the 1989 sales meeting prior to Toy Fair. The company's growth was impressive.

LEFT
*Lifestyles of the Rich
and Famous* in the 1987
catalog.

OPPOSITE
The action game
Topple was perfect for
TV promotion.

Don't Let *Topple* Topple

The 1985 catalog took a valiant stab at describing *Topple*, explaining that "Balancing acts have intrigued kids for years. And now, they can get in on the excitement with Topple. The game where winning or losing hangs in the balance of every move."

Obviously, selling the game demanded more than mere prose. It needed a good TV commercial, and in 1985, this action game became the first game of its kind Pressman promoted with a TV commercial. Jim Pressman knew he was on to something when he found *Topple* during one of his annual visits to the Toy Fair in London. It had already been successful in the UK for some years, and he wanted to transfer and magnify that success in the States.

The TV ad dramatized the action-oriented object of the game, namely, tempting and evading the risk of spectacular collapse. The commercial opened with old-timey newsreels depicting stunts performed on high buildings: a man balancing himself on the hind legs of a chair perched atop another chair atop a skyscraper, another man doing a one-handed handstand atop a lofty theater marquee. It then shifted to a group of kids having a great time playing the actual game. Astoundingly, the kid footage is just as exciting as the death-defying stuntmen seen in the opening seconds. It was enough to sell a half-million *Topple* games in the very first year.

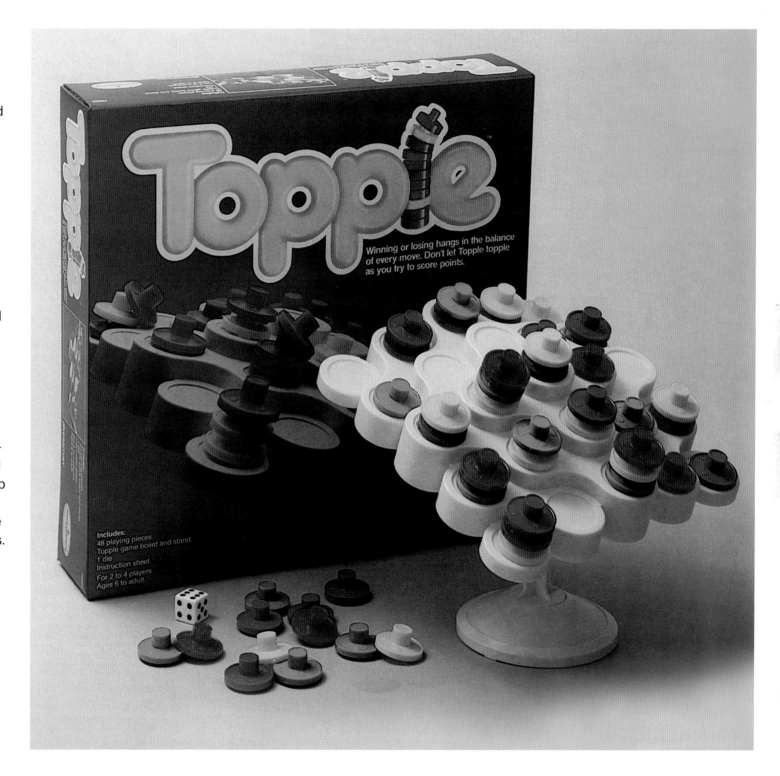

Dizzy Dizzy Dinosaur
Spins and Wins

The next successful TV-promoted action game became an even bigger hit than *Topple*. The concept had been presented to Pressman by a large inventing group out of Chicago. It was a hybrid board and action game, featuring a whirling tornado that knocks down players' pieces before they can win by being the first to complete the game.

When Jim Pressman described this to the ad agency and the Pressman design team, the concept of a tornado just did not seem quite right. A hurricane was suggested, but, like tornadoes, hurricanes are regional events, which many parts of the country never experience. Using either of these meteorological phenomena would leave large slices of the market unengaged.

What, then, is better at meting out whirling destruction than a tornado *or* a hurricane?

A whirling dinosaur! Obviously.

But what could possibly be better than a whirling dinosaur?

A *Dizzy Dizzy Dinosaur*, according to Ron Gurin, Pressman's VP of product development. And around this silly, simple, memorable name, the ad agency created a TV commercial with a jingle just catchy enough to help make the game a major hit, selling nearly one million units in one year.

Thin Ice and Jumpin' Monkeys

Thin Ice, released in 1990, and *Jumpin' Monkeys*, from 1991, were two more action games Pressman promoted on TV at the end of this period of rapid company expansion.

Thin Ice consists of a paper tissue stretched above a "water channel" filled with marbles. Using outsize tweezers, players pick up marbles and place them on the tissue, which becomes increasingly wet with each dripping marble placed there. The object is *not* to be the player whose marble breaks through the "thin ice." The TV commercial begins with penguins waddling hurriedly across Antarctic ice and then cuts to three kids having a great time actually playing the game.

Bob Fuhrer, one of the coinventors of the game, offered these thoughts: "At Nextoy, we had offices on the same (10th) floor of the iconic New York Toy Center, and we had the opportunity to share our new concepts on a regular basis. We finally struck success with a clever and inexpensive game, *Thin Ice*. This game, like many of Pressman's offerings from that golden age, has withstood the finicky whims of the toy industry and remains on the market with Goliath."

In *Jumpin' Monkeys*, players use miniature spring-loaded catapults to launch plastic monkeys into a plastic tree, with the objective of getting them to hang on a branch, monkey-style, by an arm. The player who gets all his monkeys into the tree and onto a branch wins. The TV commercial focused intently on the play, opening with the flying monkeys and then showing how the kids got them to fly. Inbar Mor Lushi Setton, the daughter of Abe Mor of Bar David Toys and Games, from which Pressman licensed *Jumpin' Monkeys*, recalled that the "game was invented by a lovely talented Frenchman, Gilbert Levy." Inbar recalled meetings at Pressman that were always "fun, natural, professional, and with great laughs." She told Jim that her father "thought highly" of him and his company.

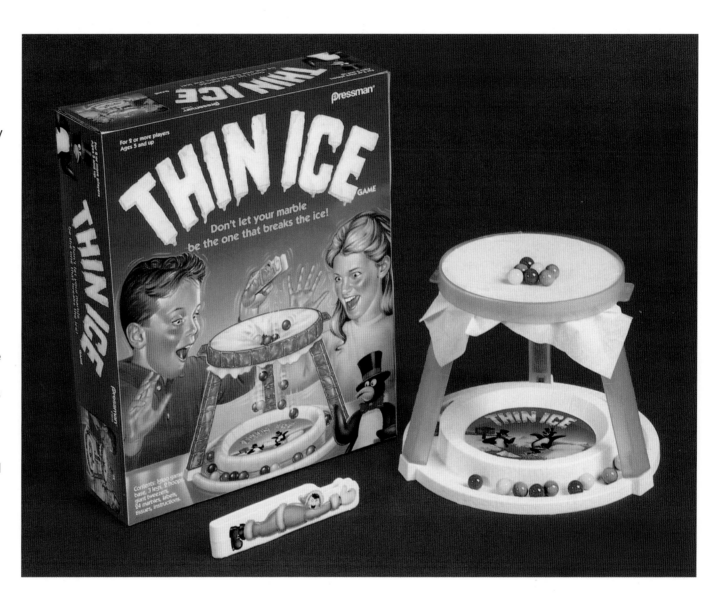

OPPOSITE
Dizzy Dizzy Dinosaur
(1987)—don't get caught in its path!

THIS PAGE
Thin Ice (1990) was a simple but highly original concept action game ideal for TV promotion.

The Checkered History of *Domino Rally*

Playing dominoes can be fun, but not as much fun as setting up long, complex rows of dominoes and then watching the chain reaction when you knock down the first domino. Add to this a spectacular combination racecourse, amusement park, and Rube Goldberg machine, and you have *Domino Rally*.

It was a game with terrific potential, which nevertheless failed to save from bankruptcy the American toy company that had first marketed it in the USA. Like Oliver Twist, *Domino Rally* was left an orphan by the collapse of its parent company, and, like Oliver Twist, it ended up on the byways of Britain, acquired by a UK company called Action GT.

On a trip to the London Toy Fair, Jim Pressman met Brian Triptree, Action GT's managing director. He showed Jim the *Domino Rally* line, which Action GT had launched in 1982. Impressed, Jim licensed the line for sale in the USA and launched it in 1989 with a remarkable TV commercial that followed the domino chain-reaction action in close-up cinematic tracking shots, at domino level. The camera really took the viewer into the action, bringing the game to life.

This kind of promotion was a big success, and *Domino Rally* took off. Over the next few years, Pressman introduced variants that featured glow-in-the-dark dominoes and slime action. The company also produced *Domino Rally* in a variety of sizes at a variety of price points. The game enjoyed a spectacular fifteen-year run.

A simple and addictive action game –
Jumpin' Monkeys (1991).

DOMINO RALLY®

The Domino Rally System combines the classic action of falling dominoes with incredible and exciting stunts! In the Basic Set, you'll find the Camelback and the Loop the Loop. Step up to the Intermediate Set and you get the Power Tower, the Camelback and the Loop the Loop. The super set features the Power Tower, the Zig Zag, the Starburst and the Rocket! And setting up all the sets is easy with the addition of specially designed "pivot" tracks. Once they're assembled, just give them a flip and they're ready to go! All the sets are compatible so that kids can collect all 3 sets and make even more elaborate Domino Rallies. For any number of players. Ages 6 and up.

No. 9501 DOMINO RALLY® BASIC SET   NEW!

Includes: 50 regular dominoes in assorted colors, 38 pivot dominoes, 2 straight paths, 1 curve track, the Camelback, the Loop the Loop, label sheet, illustrated instructions.

Packed: 12
Weight: 12 lbs.
Box size: 15⁵⁄₁₆" X 10⅜" X 2¹⁄₁₆" (Shrink wrapped)
Carton size: 12¾" X 15⅜" X 20¾"
Cube: 2.6

No. 9502 DOMINO RALLY® INTERMEDIATE SET   NEW!

Includes: 100 black dominoes, 50 pivot dominoes, 2 straight paths, 2 curve tracks, the Camelback, the Loop the Loop, the Power Tower Elevator and assembly, the Zig Zag, label sheet, illustrated instructions.

Packed: 6
Weight: 15 lbs.
Box size: 16⅝" X 11¾" X 3¼" (Shrink wrapped)
Carton size: 21" X 12¼" X 17¼"
Cube: 2.6

No. 9503 DOMINO RALLY® DELUXE SET   NEW!

Includes: 200 dominoes in assorted colors, 66 pivot dominoes, 5 straight paths, 3 curve tracks, 2 bridges, the Zig Zag, Power Tower Elevator and assembly, Rocket Launcher and assembly, Starburst, label sheet, illustrated instructions.

Packed: 6
Weight: 21 lbs.
Box size: 18¹⁄₁₆" X 14" X 3³⁄₁₆" (Shrink wrapped)
Carton size: 21" X 14½" X 18⅝"
Cube: 3.3

Domino Rally (1989) was advertised by a remarkably exciting TV spot that looked like an action feature film.

Jim and Brian Triptree do a hat trick at the Henley Royal Regatta.

Electronic Games: Armageddon for Board Games?

With the emergence of electronic gaming, the board game industry appeared to be under imminent threat of extinction or, at the very least, serious decline. Activision, Nintendo, Sega, and Sony all marketed electronic games, prompting many to doubt the future of the board game aisle. But, in time, Armageddon failed to materialize, and, against the onslaught of electronic games, board games not only survived, they thrived.

Gone Fishin'

The second half of the 1980s into the early 1990s was a time of heady innovation for Pressman Toy, but not forgotten was Jack's Pledge, that early 1950s promise that the company would never stop innovating yet also never abandon the well-loved traditional "staples."

Today, looking back at what is now a century of Pressman toys, it is clear that hardly a year went by without a fishing game or two or even more claiming space in the catalog. Over those many years, some of these games used hooks and some used magnets, but in 1987, Pressman turned on the juice with a couple of C batteries. The new game was electric, what the catalog called a "non-stop action fishing game in which players try to capture the most crabs!" The motorized game base rotated, and the mouths of the crabs opened up and snapped shut. "If you time it right, you'll be able to hook them!"

The *Let's Go Fishin'* game of 1987 was the most successful fishing game in the company's history, and it all started when Jim visited a small independent retailer called Games by James, located in the humongous Mall of America, just outside of Minneapolis. He visited the store with one of Pressman's salesmen, Mike Koewler, who sidled up to a clerk and asked what was selling. Without hesitating, she pointed to a fishing game that was being imported directly from China.

It looked totally unimpressive in its very generic, very unattractive box. But Games by James was a specialty toy store, whose staff had a face-to-face, hands-on relationship with each of its customers. The store promoted the game through employee recommendation and word of mouth.

Intrigued, Jim researched the world of fishing games. He identified certain key patents, and he identified the Chinese manufacturers who held them. Working with these companies, Pressman designers put the company's unique touch on a brand-new fishing game. Top priority for selling it was changing the packaging. Pressman made the graphics distinctive — and branded the game for its well-established Red Line of classic games.

Let's Go Fishin' just took off, and, more than three decades later, sales are still over one million pieces a year — without any TV promotion, which was never needed for this instant classic.

Let's Go Fishin' (1987) — a new iteration of the fishing games Pressman had been selling since 1932.

Let's Go Fishin'
GAME

The action fishing game where players try for the biggest catch!

⚠ **WARNING:**
CHOKING HAZARD - Small parts
Not for children under 3 years

For 1 to 4 players
Ages 4 and up
Game requires 1 size "C" battery (not included)

176

Twenty Questions—A Game and So Much More

The story of *Twenty Questions* is a story of friendship. What follows is based on the recollections of Bob Moog, the game's developer.

Bob, the young president of University Games, met Scott Mednick at a mutual friend's thirtieth birthday party. The two men conceived *Twenty Questions* as an alternative to *Trivial Pursuit*, the most popular board game of the 1980s. The trouble with *Trivial Pursuit*, Bob felt, was that many people felt stupid when they played it. Not only did they not know the answers, often they didn't even understand the questions. Bob believed an alternative would be welcome in American homes. So, he and Mednick created a game in which the answers were well known, but, to win, a player had to come up with right answers using the fewest questions.

Launched in 1987 in St. Louis, *Twenty Questions* was an immediate hit, and later that year Jim Pressman visited Bob Moog in San Francisco to ask about the possibility of licensing it from University Games. Bob was incredibly flattered, but *Twenty Questions* was University Games' bestseller! His friends and advisers were unanimous: it would be an act of absolute stupidity to license it off.

Moog, however, had an idea. He came back to Jim with three major asks. First, the license would be for US/Canada rights only, not global rights. Second, all games would feature the University Games logo on the front and back of the package in the same size as the Pressman logo. Third, Pressman needed to give University Games access to the Pressman Toy sales force as long as *Twenty Questions* was under license.

Jim, who was always willing to defy the norms of business, agreed. A handshake was made, followed by the promise of a formal contract to come. That is where the trouble started. On December 28, before the contracts were received, Bob got a call from Phil Orbanes, head of product acquisition at Parker Brothers. He had received *Twenty Questions* as a Christmas present and loved it. Within forty-eight hours, Bob Moog had a draft Parker Brothers contract in his hands, and his partner, Cris Lehman, began negotiations with that company. Bob called Jim right after New Year's, but Jim was overseas at the Toy Show in Hong Kong and not available.

By January 5, Bob had two confirmed deals for *Twenty Questions* and knew that someone would be disappointed or worse. During the second week of January, Bob went to Toronto for the annual Canadian Toy Fair and was shocked to see samples of *Twenty Questions* on display and offered for sale at the Parker Brothers booth — without his company's logo. He called Orbanes since no licensing deal had been executed. Apologetically, Phil said that it must be some kind of mistake. It was enough, however, to shift the decision to Pressman Toy, and the deal was consummated — for less money — in January 1988.

In fact, the *Twenty Questions* business license proved to be a license of friendship between Bob Moog and Jim Pressman. For the next three years, Jim welcomed Bob and his team into the Pressman family and served as a mentor and coach to Bob, who attended sales meetings and had full access to the Pressman offices — including free hot dogs at Toy Fair. (Well, everybody there got the hot dogs for free.)

Bob also attended meetings at Toy Fair with key customers. His best memory from the 1988 Toy Fair was when Jim and Bob presented *Twenty Questions* to an important game buyer, who liked the game and said he would try it. As he walked away, Jim looked at Bob, did a little jump, and let out a quiet "Yippee."

Pressman Toy generated hundreds of thousands of dollars in royalties for University Games from 1988 to 1992. The game eventually ran its course and reverted to University Games, but the friendship between the Pressman family and the Moog family has been going strong for some thirty years. As for University Games, defying the long odds against startup game makers, it continues to be a dynamic and successful company both in the US and internationally.

A Deal and a Friendship Begins on a Napkin

In 1987, Adi Golad and his father visited the Pressman Toy showroom at Toy Fair. Following this visit, Adi and Jim began discussions about licensing *Tri-Ominos* to Goliath Toys for distribution in Holland. They completed the negotiation a few days later in a small Lebanese restaurant and signed off on terms scribbled on a paper napkin. The licensing deal between Pressman and Goliath seeded the friendship and commercial relations between the Pressmans and the Golads. In 1989, *Tri-Ominos* was awarded Toy of the Year in the tiny Netherlands.

In the following years, Jim and Donna and their daughter, Kate, became very close to Adi and his wife, Margreeth, and their four children. They even visited them in their home in Holland. Some twenty-five years later, after Goliath had opened a company in the USA, Adi learned of Jim's intent to sell the family business (more on this in chapter 17).

OPPOSITE
A new take on "the original American parlor game," *Twenty Questions* (1988).

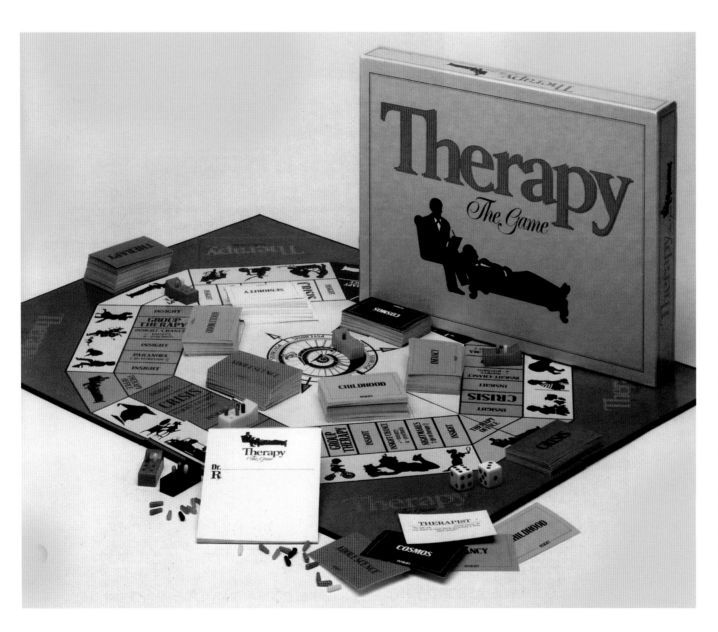

Therapy: Another Love Story

"Games people play. Together" was not just Press-man's tagline during the 1980s. It was a new basic philosophy of game making, which looked at games as being a way to get people together, to have fun together, and to get to know others across a game board. Even in business itself, a company like Press-man ran on creating, growing, and sustaining relationships. The deal between University Games and Pressman had nearly died. But it didn't. And, years later, Bob Moog credited the survival of University Games to the deal with Pressman.

Which brings us to *Therapy: The Game*. It was the brainchild of three inventors, one of whom was a practicing psychiatrist. Billed as an "exciting, hilarious, and revealing game," it asked such provocative questions as "So tell me, which player would be the *least* embarrassed buying a ticket to an erotic movie?" To win the game, "players answer questions in the six stages of life, and by curing other players in therapy or group therapy."

The game didn't actually guarantee a cure, but it

did promise this much: "You never know what you will learn" when you play *Therapy*.

Before Pressman licensed it in 1986, *Therapy* had had moderate success in its original run with the copyright owner, a small company called Gambit Games. It was decidedly an adult game because, in therapy, after all, questions sometimes contain sexual content. That meant that big-box stores like Toys"R"Us insisted on putting a "burst" on the box containing a warning that it was for adults only. Doubtless, this did not serve so much to caution potential buyers as it did to convert prospects into purchasers.

At about this time, Jim met a woman named Donna when she and a couple of her girlfriends visited his house on Long Island. Jim had *Therapy: The Game* in the house, and when Donna took an interest in it, he gave it to her as an impromptu gift. In this way, *Therapy* played a modest but notable part in a blossoming romance. While, for most couples, romance begins with a first date, for Jim and Donna, it was a game that brought them together, and, five years later, they married.

OPPOSITE
Therapy – the game that changed Jim's life.

LEFT
Jim and Donna Pressman in 2019.

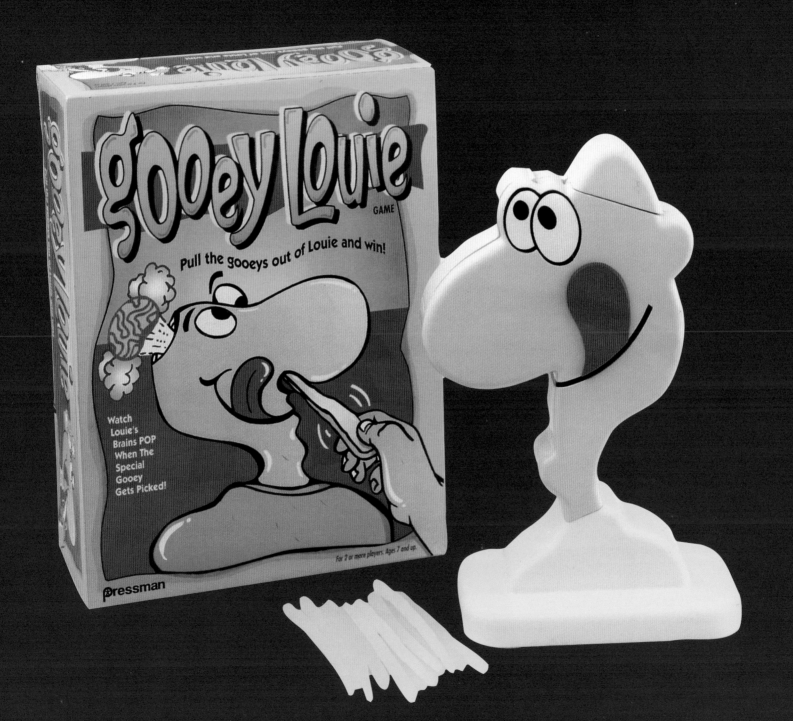

Pressman's *Gooey Louie* (1995) boldly went where no game had gone before.

Chapter 14
Rule Breakers
1992–1998

Like many specialized industries, the game and toy business operated according to certain generally accepted norms. The larger companies were the most reluctant to challenge these unwritten rules, but Pressman didn't answer to public shareholders. In fact, it reported only to one authority, its key customers: the kids.

Digging for Boogers and Finding Gold

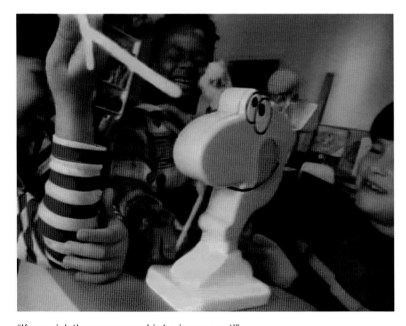

Pressman's TV commercial for *Gooey Louie* proudly proclaimed that the game was "Gross!"

"If you pick the wrong one, his brains pop out!"

Under Jim Pressman, the company placed a lot of bets, but when something looked like a long shot — high reward, high risk — Jim usually hedged his bets with a focus group. Pressman would call in its advertising agency to recruit and convene groups of kids who would play the game or games the company was developing or thinking about developing. Jim and other decision makers, including the ad agency's account executives, observed the action from the other side of a one-way mirror. They would also monitor any question-and-answer session that followed play.

A lot that was good or bad about a game became apparent just from watching the kids play, but when they were asked what they wanted, the executives hung on their every word. Luckily, the kids always spoke loudly and clearly about what they liked and did not like.

A case in point: in 1995, the company tested a game called *Gooey Louie* with one of these focus groups. No question about it, it was an instant hit with the kids. Pressman urgently needed to see this response before investing in a game that had as its object not solving a puzzle or defeating a chess master but pulling snot out of a character's nose.

The focus group demonstrated what Jim and the others suspected. Louie's nose was *so* gross that it could not help but be *so* much fun.

Actually, Pressman was not the first company to focus-test this game, but it was the first to make an offer. Was it a stroke of genius that the Pressman decision makers saw what others in other companies (Milton Bradley, Mattel, Parker Brothers, and Tyco among them) could not see?

Perhaps . . . but, more likely, it was that those other companies tested the game with kids and their parents together, behind the one-way glass. Apparently, the kids knew better than to announce in front of their moms and dads that they loved nothing more than picking boogers out of a nose, any nose. So in those tests for other companies, they didn't vote thumbs-up on the game.

It says a lot about Pressman at this time that no one in the company even proposed testing the game in the presence of parents. As far as Pressman Toy was concerned, the only role parents played in a focus group was to bring their kids in, drop them off at the test site, and then pick them up about an hour later. Left on their own, kids would let you know what they really wanted. And, left on their own, what they really wanted was to put their fingers up the nose of *Gooey Louie*.

The inventing organization behind *Gooey Louie* was Meyer Glass, a Chicago-based group spun off from the legendary Marvin Glass toy-inventing company. As Steve Meyer recalled, "The idea was inspired by one of the designers after a dream he had during the allergy season."

So, Pressman bought the game and started making it. Whatever else *Gooey Louie* was, it was an *action* game, and, by this time, Pressman knew very well how to advertise action games. Without question, it had to be on TV.

The commercial focused on kid after kid pulling a "gooey" from Louie's nose. "But if you pick the wrong gooey," the voiceover announcer warned, "Gooey Louie's brains pop out." And *that* was the secret of the game and the commercial. Just when you thought things couldn't get any grosser, they did.

Today, there are games that include poop, doggy doodoo, toilet flushing, and many other highly impolite things. But *Gooey Louie* was the first of its kind. When it came into the Pressman offices, it was called *Snot Face*. That seemed a bit too much, so Pressman changed the name. While *Gooey Louie* was more euphonious than *Snot Face*, it was not any more polite.

And that was the point. The delight of playing *Gooey Louie* was not in being gross for the sake of grossness but being given license to violate an almost-sacred taboo. Since time out of mind, adults have commanded children, *Don't pick your nose!* And now, after untold millennia, came a game whose very object was to disobey.

It went on to national and international success. Boogers were going global in the nineties, and they continue to do so to this very day.

Breaking the Indoor Water Taboo

One of the longest-standing and, from all appearances, least breakable rules in the world of toys decrees that outdoor games are outdoor games and indoor games are indoor games and never the twain shall meet.

In 1997, Pressman exuberantly broke the indoor-outdoor rule with *Hydro Strike!*

As everyone knew, playing with water was tolerated outdoors but strictly off-limits indoors. And this was for good and obvious reasons. No parent (or landlord) would stand for such a thing! So, naturally, the people at Pressman could not resist breaking or at least bending this rule.

Given the magnitude of the taboo, Pressman focus-group tested *Hydro Strike!* As the 1997 catalog subsequently boasted, this "thrilling head-to-head pinball-action game features the biggest payoff you've ever seen!" But first, you had to pump up the game's tank to load the water and then place the ball on the release ramp. The next step (the catalog explained) was to "grip your handles and send the ball speeding down the alley towards your opponent's goal. When you hit his target, the most *striking* feature of *Hydro Strike!* is activated. He gets sprayed with the Hydro-Mist. When he hits his button the mist stops immediately, but you score the point."

It was "Win . . . or get WET!"

But while the winner won, nobody really lost, because the loser got something even better — the experience of being sprayed. In fact, in testing, Pressman found that kids actually preferred losing to winning so that they could savor an experience no other indoor toy ever gave them: getting wet.

The sensation of breaking an ultimate household

The *Hydro Strike!* action game made a splash in the 1997 Pressman catalog.

taboo against water was irresistible, and, promoted by a highly effective TV commercial, *Hydro Strike!* enjoyed widespread buyer acceptance that continues to this day.

Astoundingly, Pressman encountered no protest from buyers. Well, except for Walmart, and because Walmart was such a whale of a customer, Jim flew down to Walmart HQ in Bentonville, Arkansas, to personally convince the buyer that parents would pick up the game for their children, water and all.

It turned out to be a hard sell, which called for a compromise. The Walmart buyer surrendered, agreeing to write a substantial order on condition that Pressman include on the packaging a prominent blurb that described a "light spray" of water. From Jim's perspective, the statement, intended to overcome any parental resistance by minimizing the apparent volume of the spray, had the opposite effect. It *overstated* the spray, drawing attention to it. And that was just fine with him.

Hydro Strike! performed beyond Pressman's highest hopes for it. Over three hundred thousand pieces sold in one year, and it also did very well internationally. This was no accident, as the inventor of the game, Eddy Goldfarb — one hundred years old at this writing — is still considered one of the best game inventors in the toy industry. As big a hit as *Hydro Strike!* was, Eddy is far more famous for having invented in 1949 one of the all-time novelty classics: *Yakity Yak Talking Teeth*, generically known as *Chattering Teeth*.

Ring Around the Nosy

Not everything Pressman did during the nineties deliberately broke rules. In 1993 the company revisited one of the most traditional of party games, "bobbing for apples," but with a twist that came via an inventing group from the UK. Seven Towns, the company was called, and its wizards had figured out a way to convert the idea of bobbing for apples into an original toy.

In the British Isles, Seven Towns licensed their game successfully as *Doughnutters.* It consisted of an elephant mask from which a long, upturned elephant's trunk protruded, a game board, and a set of thick plastic rings to be piled on the board. The object was to use the elephant's trunk to hook as many of the rings as possible. It wasn't easy to get the blunt trunk under the ring to flip it up off the board. Players had to go bobbing for the stubborn rings. According to Mike Moody of Seven Towns, "the game evolved from an idea submitted by Hans Ulrich, a German inventor of crazy toys."

Jim found *Doughnutters* at the UK Toy Fair. He loved the concept from the get-go, but the name, *Doughnutters,* seemed a non-starter. In collaboration with its ad agency, Pressman came up with a completely different name – *Ring Around the Nosy* – and a memorable TV spot, which simply showed kids having a great time bobbing for rings with an earworm of a jingle playing in voiceover.

Like many others with whom Jim Pressman did business, Mike Moody enjoyed working with the company. "Jim was always a gentleman to deal with and put his heart into making products successful. We shared the ups and downs over the years, but without doubt he's one of the best. We will never forget the wonderful hospitality and tour open to us every Toy Fair in the old Toy Center of the World."

Ring Around the Nosy (1993) was bobbing for apples, but with an elephant mask.

An unlikely TV license, the *Saved by the Bell* game was a big hit, especially among the female tween set.

TV Spawns a Different Kind of Game

As early as the 1960s, Pressman well understood that games and television naturally go together. Translating a certain TV game show into an action game or even a board game was sometimes so evident a choice that it was practically in your face, like a thrown pie. But mining other types of TV fare could offer less obvious but still potentially profitable ore.

Saved by the Bell, which premiered on NBC in 1989 and ran until 1993, followed the lives of some high school friends in Los Angeles. The show never had monster ratings, but it did command a loyal cohort of very committed fans, especially tween girls, who really – *really* – liked the male leads, Mark-Paul Gosselaar and Mario Lopez. That drew Jim's attention, along with the fact that girls are more apt to buy a board game than boys. Coincidentally, the show's producer,

Peter Engel, had been a counselor at the summer camp Jim had gone to as a kid. And Lynn Pressman was a good friend of Peter's mother. Neither of these incidentals drove the decision to license a game, but any connection is valuable for starting a discussion.

Jim was also well aware that some of Pressman's competitors were bringing out girl-oriented games based on boy bands. So the market had been demonstrated, and it seemed like a good time to get into it. Some suggested that the whole appeal of the boy-band games was just a way for girls to get pictures of cute celebrity boys. Maybe that would be the real appeal of a game based on *Saved by the Bell*.

So what if it was? Jim called NBC, made a proposal, and then a deal.

Zoom Ball—Faster than a Rocket Ship (Maybe)

Ah, spring! Who doesn't love spring?

Game companies.

It is hardly a trade secret that winter, a gift-giving season whose centerpiece is Christmas, is the high point of the toy industry's year. Spring? Not so much. Back in 1964, Pressman had its very first spring break-out TV success story with the giant "invisible" *Superman Kite*, but the second spring TV breakout did not come until 1993.

That was when Jerry Smith, president of Playtoy, the Canadian toymaker that had licensed the highly successful *Trivia Adventure* to Pressman in 1984 (see chapter 12), called on Jim in Pressman Toy's New York office.

Jerry was excited. He wanted to demonstrate something he had found: *Zoom Ball*. It consisted of a vaguely football-shaped ball through which two lines ran. Players gripped handles on the ends of the two lines, and when a player pulled the handles apart, the *Zoom Ball* became what the Pressman catalog called "a rocketful of speed."

It was not an exaggeration – at least not from a player's perspective. Indeed, just one zip of the *Zoom Ball* from Jerry's hands to Jim's was all it took to sell Pressman's president on the game. For it was a toy that delivered a genuinely visceral experience. You had this "shockingly colorful" ball on a string with two handles on your side and two handles on the other side. When you pulled the two handles apart, the ball zoomed over to the other player.

It was incredibly fast! It was also very safe. Yet the thrill was that nothing about *Zoom Ball* seemed safe. And so it was yet another rule breaker.

The deal was made, and Pressman launched *Zoom Ball* with a TV campaign that featured frenetic seconds of play intercut with slow-motion scenes of other games, such as jump rope, which looked very dull by contrast. The game immediately became that rarest of phenomena: the breakout toy for spring.

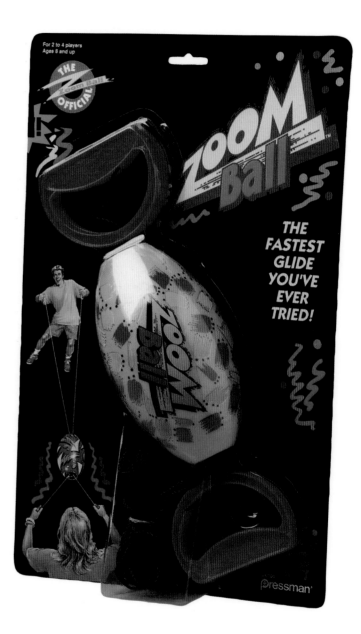

The Official Zoom Ball (1993*)* was incredibly fast and remarkably intense yet perfectly safe.

Trolling for Treasure

A movie version of the popular *Addams Family* TV show came out in 1991 and earned $10 million in a single day. A sequel was soon announced — and, in between, Pressman came out with *The Addams Family Family Reunion Game*, a licensed product.

In the 1930s, Pressman capitalized on licenses from such comic strips as *Little Orphan Annie* and the *Dick Tracy* radio show. In the 1950s, the company turned to television with shows that featured the likes of Groucho Marx and children's comic Pinky Lee.

Now, in the 1990s, licensing expanded to movies, such as *Addams Family Values*; books, among them

the then-popular *For Dummies* series of how-to manuals; TV shows, including the likes of *Saved by the Bell*; and even popular toy lines from other toy companies.

Such was the case with *Trolls*.

These were dolls with big ears and eyes, a pug nose, and, typically, a broad but pleasingly grotesque smile, as well as a thatch of up-combed furry hair. The brainchildren of Thomas Dam, a Danish woodcutter,

For 2 to 4 players
Ages 5 and up

Treasure Trolls ™

Search for the Wishstones Game

Pressman®

4 Treasure Trolls™ Inside!

Contents: 4 - 1" Treasure Trolls™ (colors may vary)
Gameboard • Wishstone™ jewel die • Instructions

Trolls were first marketed as toys in 1959. During the early 1960s, *Trolls* swept the world.

After briefly dying down later in the 1960s, the *Troll* fad resurged in the 1970s through the 1990s, and various companies introduced licensed spinoffs, including video games and TV shows. Pressman hopped on the *Troll* train in 1992 with a game based on *Treasure Trolls*, which were being manufactured and marketed by ACE Novelties. This species of troll was distinguished from the others by the little jewel in its navel. Acting on a tip from a friend in the advertising business, Allen Bohbot, Jim licensed *Treasure Trolls* for a board game that would be a treasure hunt in which four miniature *Treasure Trolls* were the moving pieces.

"Treasure Trolls are going to be really hot," Jim's tipster friend told him. And they were!

Treasure Trolls were popular variations on the original Troll doll toys. Pressman licensed these little figures for the Treasure Trolls Search for the Wishstones Game and Treasure Tolls Match-Up Card Game in 1993.

A beloved member of the Pressman Toy Corporation family, Herbert G. Lane died much too soon, in February 1997, just as that year's Toy Fair was getting underway.

Family Is Still Part of the Business

During the 1990s, Toy Fair was held once a year in what were collectively known as the Toy Buildings, at 200 Fifth Avenue and 1107 Broadway, New York City. The Pressman showroom was on the tenth floor of the Fifth Avenue building. The space was roomy, equipped as the company's headquarters, with regular offices, including, at one end, Jim Pressman's office and those of the VP of marketing, R & D, and the art department. At the other end of the company's space was a showroom, which was used for just two weeks out of the year during Toy Fair and lay idle for the rest of the year.

For Jim, thoughts of Toy Fair bring up all sorts of warm memories of great business relationships. Herb Lane, a nephew of Lynn, was a key salesperson for the company. It was Herb's father, Moe Lane, who had been responsible for introducing Lynn to Jack. Herb joined the company in 1962. He was a big and gentle man loved by all. It was Herb who took Jim to his first baseball game at Ebbets Field, to see the beloved Brooklyn Dodgers. And it was also Herb who took Jim on his first airplane trip to Washington, DC, to see the 1956 Baseball All-Star Game. Jim will never forget the day that Herb came into his office at the beginning of one Toy Fair just to tell him what a great job he was doing as the head of the firm. No one else said such a thing, at least not with such warmth and sincerity.

Herb passed away at his home on the morning of February 1, 1997, just as Toy Fair meetings were beginning. For everyone who knew him, it was a shockingly sudden end to a beautiful life. Jim could hardly believe that the 1997 Toy Fair would go on without him.

Marketing with Relish

Toy Fair was a time that buyers from all over the country and the world came to see the new products that would be coming out in the months that followed. Buyers could be enticed to showrooms for many reasons. But Pressman had something that no one else had.

At lunchtime during Toy Fair, Lynn Pressman started what became a Pressman tradition. She hired an icon of Manhattan street life, a Sabrett Hot Dogs cart, brought it into the showroom, and served hot dogs, complete with all the fixings, to hungry buyers.

The aroma drifted out into the hallway, inviting buyers to make certain they booked a Pressman tour. And they did, taking care to make it sometime around lunchtime. The Pressman showroom was always active during Toy Fair, but it was strictly standing room only at lunchtime — until the Toy Fair moved to the mammoth Javits Center in 2000.

Toy Fair was all about business-to-business marketing, but, at its best, it was also personal, and Lynn's genius here was to realize that getting a classic Manhattan hot dog was the perfect personal vehicle for handselling intensely competitive merchandise.

Breaking bread has always been a way of bonding, but being served a delicious hot dog from a cart that was usually on a street corner was a token of a special, even unique, relationship. Other toymakers might offer sandwiches and the like, but these could hardly compete with the pungent aroma of a Sabrett dog with mustard, sauerkraut, and neon-green relish. It is quite possible that some buyers came for the hot dogs and stayed for the toys.

Hot dog marketing was a feature of the very special

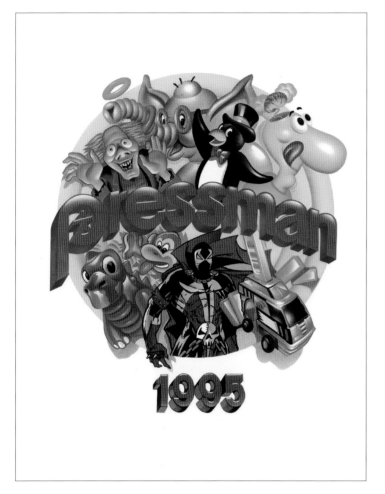

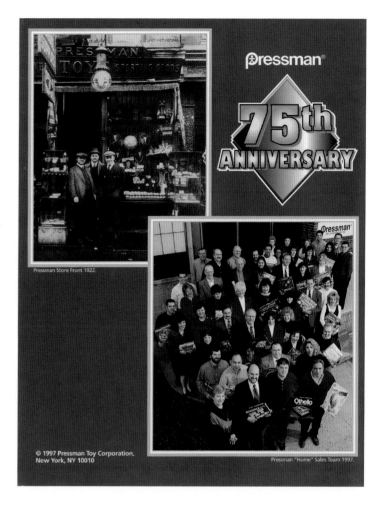

way of doing business that characterized the otherwise often cutthroat toy business in those days. Whatever else compelled buyers to write an order, a strong relationship was what ultimately closed the sale. And that New York hot dog, fully dressed, was the secret sauce. After Jim became president, he changed the dynamics of the business in many ways, but he never gave up serving the hot dogs.

Catalog front covers from 1995 and 1996, and the back cover from 1997 – the seventy-fifth anniversary of Pressman Toy Corporation.

Chapter 15
Who Wants to Be a Millionaire?

2000

It is hard to imagine what Jack Pressman may have envisioned for his company's future when he passed away in 1959 with annual sales just under $2 million. In the year 2000, Pressman Toy shipped $2 million — in just one day. This was courtesy of its home game version of the TV game-show sensation *Who Wants to Be a Millionaire?*

PRESSMAN BRINGS HOME

THE EXCITEMENT, THE TENSION OF T.V.'S HOTTEST GAME SHOW PHENOMENON...

New!

It's the most excitement to hit TV game shows in years AND the most excitement to hit the game aisles in decades!

Based on the mega-hit game show, this brand new home version has all the elements that make the TV game show the powerhouse success that it is!

Each player gets to act as host while the other players try to win more and more money by answering entertaining and amusing questions using their own hand-held card consoles.
Stuck for an answer?
Use the Lifelines just like they do on TV!

Ask the host to delete two incorrect answers from your card console. Now you can choose one from the two remaining answers!

50:50

Ask the audience! The other players will show you what they think is the right answer... well, at least you HOPE that's what they're showing you!

You can even phone a friend, hope that they're home and... that they know the correct answer!

Keep your stack of money growing and— if you get to be the millionaire- or the player with the most money at the end of the game- you win!

15	$1 MILLION
14	$500,000
13	$250,000
12	$125,000
11	$64,000
10	$32,000
9	$16,000
8	$8,000
7	$4,000
6	$2,000
5	$1,000
4	$500
3	$300
2	$200
1	$100

#5000-04 WHO WANTS TO BE A MILLIONAIRE

For 2 to 5 players, ages 12 to adult.

Packed: 4	Weight: 19 lbs.	Cube: 1.2
Box Size: 14" x 10.38" x 3" (shrink wrapped)		Carton Size: 14.38" x 11.25" x 12.75"

Contents: 1000 Cards (over 1900 questions), 5 Question and Answer Card Consoles, Lots of Money, Lifeline Tokens, Instructions

UPC No. 0-21853-05000-4

Produced under license from Celador Productions Limited.

2

Presenting...
the TOTY Awards for 2000

The saga of Pressman's *Millionaire* game culminated on a night in February 2001 at the Cipriani Event Space on 42nd Street in Midtown Manhattan. It was the night that the toy industry celebrated its first annual TOTY Awards. An acronym for Toy Of The Year, the TOTY was intended to be the industry's equivalent of the film industry's Oscar.

That night, *Who Wants to Be a Millionaire?* won TOTYs for both Game of the Year and License of the Year. There were very good reasons for both awards.

Licensing a Winner

Jim Pressman negotiated the rights to the *Millionaire* game from Celador, the UK-based entertainment company that produced *Who Wants to Be a Millionaire?* for TV. Celador's head of marketing explained why his company chose Pressman Toy as a licensee for one of its most valuable properties: "We were looking for a company that would maintain the integrity of the show and give it the attention to detail that it deserves. Given their demonstrated success within the game industry and the passion they brought to the project, Pressman was our first choice."

In truth, the process of capturing this important license was not quite so quick and simple as these two flattering sentences imply. Paul Smith, Celador's founder, visited Jim at his New York offices in 1999. He was following up on the recommendation of Upstarts, the UK company that held the rights to *Millionaire* in the UK. The people at Upstarts had gotten to know and trust Jim Pressman through repeated encounters with him at the London Toy Fair, and they did not hesitate to recommend Pressman Toy to Smith.

Now, a company's good name goes very far in the toy business, but it's not everything. There is also money involved. In the case of the *Millionaire* license, it was a lot of money, and when Paul Smith asked for a $250,000 guarantee – a very hefty and totally non-refundable advance against sales-based royalties – Jim was more than a bit taken back. It was a far larger advance than his company had ever paid.

Smith responded to Jim's skepticism by making a compelling case for that very substantial guarantee. He had the facts and figures to demonstrate the success of *Millionaire* in the UK and other markets worldwide, and he promised it would have the same success in the US. Based on experience, Jim believed him. So, swallowing hard, he smiled, shook hands, and agreed to the deal.

Top 15 Selling Items Introduced in 2000 Only

Ranked by dollars and based on March sales

1 Pokémon Jungle Pack/*Wizards Of The Coast*
Introduced: Feb. '00   Avg. retail price: $3.19

2 Who Wants To Be A Millionare/*Pressman*
Introduced: Feb. '00   Avg. retail price: $29.17

3 Wuv Luv Asst./*Trendmasters*
Introduced: Feb. '00   Avg. retail price: $28.00

4 Barbie Wizard Of Oz Asst./*Mattel*
Introduced: Feb. '00   Avg. retail price: $12.95

5 Digimon Cards/*Bandai America*
Introduced: Jan. '00   Avg. retail price: $9.31

6 Pokémon Base Set/*Wizards Of The Coast*
Introduced: Feb. '00   Avg. retail price: $9.89

7 Barbie Hawaii With Bucket/*Mattel*
Introduced: Jan. '00   Avg. retail price: $4.75

8 Starting Line-Up 2000 MLB All-Stars Asst./*Hasbro*
Introduced: Feb. '00   Avg. retail price: $7.87

9 Powerpuff Doll/Sound Asst./*Trendmasters*
Introduced: Jan. '00   Avg. retail price: $7.53

10 New Wave Hoop/*Maui Toys*
Introduced: Jan. '00   Avg. retail price: $5.56

11 Wizard Of Oz Men Asst./*Mattel*
Introduced: Feb. '00   Avg. retail price: $18.40

12 Digimon DX Fingerboards/*Bandai America*
Introduced: Feb. '00   Avg. retail price: $5.01

13 Endless Bubbles/*Tootsietoy*
Introduced: Jan. '00   Avg. retail price: $5.97

14 Digimon Box/*Upper Deck*
Introduced: Jan. '00   Avg. retail price: $19.92

15 Gooze Asst./*Flying Colors*
Introduced: Jan. '00   Avg. retail price: $4.67

Who Wanted to Be a Millionaire? Turns Out, Lots and Lots of People

Who Wants to Be a Millionaire? started airing on British television in September 1998 and was adapted for the US market from the UK original by Michael Davies, a US-based British TV game-show producer. The show was – and remains – a straightforward quiz competition in which contestants aim for a million-dollar top prize by answering multiple-choice questions of increasing difficulty. Each question is worth a specific amount of money, but when a contestant gives a wrong answer, the game is over. Depending which of three progressive tiers the contestant has reached in the game, the loss may result in walking away with absolutely nothing or with some amount that is very considerably less than $1 million. All in all, the progress of play makes for a highly suspenseful and dramatic scenario.

The American premiere of *Millionaire* was on August 16, 1999, hosted by Regis Philbin, a veteran talk-show, news-show, and game-show host. In *Millionaire*, Regis found his perfect game-show fit. The chemistry was magic, the show was great, and *Who Wants to Be a Millionaire?* was a skyrocket. Practically overnight it became the highest-rated primetime game show in TV history.

Looking back, the stats are still staggering. An astonishing thirty million viewers tuned in three nights a week to watch – and, some weeks, the show aired as many as *five* times! So what could possibly go wrong with a board game built on success like this?

Theoretically, absolutely nothing.

In reality, however, sales of the game in 2000 were alarmingly sluggish. It was by no means a flop, just a disappointment – a profound disappointment, given Pressman's stratospheric retail expectations.

Yet just as the TV game itself was built on the deliciously unbearable suspense of a succession of all-or-nothing decisions, so the fate of Pressman's *Millionaire* was a cliff-hanger. At long last, sales momentum began to pick up and then accelerate, continuing to churn faster and faster through the holiday season, so that by the end of a year that had begun slowly, the home version of *Who Wants to Be a Millionaire?* was the fourth-bestselling *toy* of the year. More significantly, it was the *number one* bestselling *game* – not just in the USA but the whole world.

For good reason, then, Pressman Toy captured two TOTYs and was named Licensee of the Year by LIMA, the Licensing Industry Merchandisers' Association. Jim Pressman was personally honored as Entrepreneur of the Year by no less than the venerable Ernst and Young consulting firm.

Even more tangible awards came at checkout counters worldwide. The game sold over three million pieces in its first year, and sales of the Pressman Toy Corporation doubled to $98 million in 2000 from $45 million the year before. In 2001, Pressman built on its success by creating a highly successful *Millionaire* junior edition for younger kids.

Dieter Strehl, managing director of the venerable Viennese maker of playing cards and board games Piatnik, recalls the "phenomenal success of *Who Wants to Be a Millionaire?* . . . Pressman sold an incredible number in the US, and we – on a much smaller scale – in Austria, Hungary, and Slovenia. We spoke a lot about this item, about manufacturing and how best to advertise it. In the beginning, sales were slow, but at the end it became one of the most successful games in the world! Over the years, Jim and Donna became friends of ours and also visited us in Vienna. We once went together with their daughter, Kate, to the Vienna Zoo, one of the oldest zoos in the world, and had a lot of fun in the cage with the bats!"

High Water Mark

The *Who Wants to Be a Millionaire?* home game was introduced on the cusp of a revolution in gaming. Digital games were still in their infancy. In 2000, there were no electronic tabletop games or any other digital versions of *Who Wants to Be a Millionaire?* to compete with Pressman's board game. It was clear to Jim, however, that this would surely change in the coming years. He also knew that the phenomenal success of *Millionaire* would be hard to duplicate in a gaming universe that was just entering the early stages of disruption by such digital platforms as Nintendo, Xbox, and PlayStation, as well as by games designed to be played on PCs, Macs, and mobile phones.

This is not to say that the era of the board game was at an end. On the contrary, Jim was confident that board games would continue to be a profitable business. It was just that the era of monster board game hits was slipping away. That was the new reality. *Millionaire*, a great game, would not last forever. In fact, at the very height of demand for *Millionaire*,

Jim, with one eye on the future, looked for ways to increase production to meet current demand without investing in permanent expansion. By offering employees overtime for longer hours and acquiring additional warehouse space, Pressman Toy was able to double its manufacturing output with no new purchases of equipment or hiring of additional personnel.

Recognizing that *Millionaire* represented a high-water mark in the traditional game industry, Jim knew that those waters, so warm and inviting at the moment, were about to recede. He refused to make the mistake competitors were making, putting a permanent investment into an expansion to meet temporary demand.

At this time, Jim set up two computer programs to monitor sales. One program was dedicated solely to *Millionaire*, while the other tracked everything else. He knew that once *Millionaire* had run its course, the core of the company would remain, and the dual-tracking system would make it easier to analyze trends as *Millionaire* diminished as a driver.

OPPOSITE
In June 2000, *Playthings* listed *Who Wants to Be a Millionaire?* as the second-bestselling toy introduced that year, behind only *Pokémon Jungle Pack*.

ABOVE
In a Manhattan gala on June 13, 2001, the Licensing Industry Merchandisers' Association (LIMA) named Pressman Toy Corporation its 2001 Licensee of the Year, thanks to the phenomenal success of *Millionaire*. Jim accepted the honor.

February 10, 2001, saw the first annual TOTY Awards presentation. Invitation was by ticket only, and that night, *Who Wants to Be a Millionaire?* won TOTYs for both Game of the Year and License of the Year. Jim accepted both.

Life Is Beautiful

Just because highwater times are not forever, it does not mean that those majestic peaks are mere mirages. They are fun, they are thrilling, and they are real, even if they don't last as long as you would like them to.

Jim put his heart into his TOTY acceptance speech:

We are honored to have won this award and want to thank all the TMA members for this honor. It is especially meaningful because it validates our belief in the continued relevance and vitality of traditional board games in today's high-tech society.

In Pressman's seventy-nine years, we have had our share of successes – but never anything as big as *Millionaire.* I want to thank all the retailers who supported us – and the key executives of Pressman Toy who happen to be here tonight who dedicate themselves to our business – David Shapiro, Joe Spina, Gail Jackman, and Mark Koscinski, and to their wives, husbands, and friends who support them. And I want to say a special thank-you to my wife, Donna, who is always there for me. And one last special thank-you to Celador – the greatest production company and licensor in the world, who make all this possible. Thanks, Katherine.

Thank you all. And long live the board game!

Jim Silver, a writer for the toy trade magazines, wrote of the night of the TOTY Awards: "Special kudos to Jim Pressman of Pressman Games, now known as the Roberto Benigni of the toy business."

Benigni was the irrepressible director and star of the 1997 Italian comedy-drama *Life Is Beautiful.* It was a movie that grossed $230 million worldwide and $57.6 million in the US alone, winning three Oscars, including Best Foreign Language Film and Best Actor. Benigni's joyously exuberant acceptance of his Oscars was a sensation, reported in headlines and endlessly repeated on shows like *Entertainment Tonight.*

"Jim's excitement was contagious and electrifying, yet he was humble while winning two deserved awards," Jim Silver wrote, and the cherry on the sundae of that TOTY night was the identity of the two men who presented Jim Pressman with the Game of the Year TOTY. They were George Ditomassi and George Volonakis, top executives at Pressman's arch competitor, the mighty Hasbro Toy Company.

Pressman Toy did what it had always done. It continued to innovate, and the new century would bring many new and diverse licenses. But Jack's Pledge from the 1950s still held true. The company continued to balance innovation with the classic games, the "staples" that had lives measurable in decades, not just seasons.

Pressman for the new millennium – the 2000 catalog cover.

BASED ON THE HIT TV SHOW!

DEAL or NO DEAL

THE BOARD GAME

AS SEEN ON
NBC

Designed for 2 to 6 players

Pressman

Pressman's *Deal or No Deal* board game (2005).

Chapter 16
Playing and Winning in the New Millennium

1999–2014

At the dawn of a new century – in fact, a new millennium – a host of new media emerged or matured. Having pioneered licensing in the toy and game industries, Pressman now inaugurated expanded licensing and promotional programs, looking to capitalize on fresh trends in traditional media as well as evolving interactive media.

New Millennium, New Media Opportunities

For years after the emergence of broadcast television in the early 1950s, three major national networks had ruled the airwaves, with larger cities supplementing these by one or two local stations and "educational television," which became PBS.

Cable TV was developed alongside broadcast television as a service for remote areas that could not receive TV over the air. By the 1980s, however, cable began offering competitive alternatives to broadcast network fare. These alternatives multiplied through the 1990s and by the beginning of the new millennium became truly formidable competition for the traditional broadcast networks. As we saw in chapter 13, Pressman licensed a *Double Dare* action game from the kid's game show featured on an upstart cable network called Nickelodeon. It was a smash. As more and more kid-friendly cable shows proliferated in the 1990s and into the 2000s, Jim Pressman made more deals.

The mid-1990s saw the rise of the internet, which spawned various interactive games, ripe for licensing. A would-be licensee had to be both savvy and careful, however, because the internet had a way of giving birth to faddish one-hit wonders as well as games with substantial legs.

Even as new media proliferated, Jim Pressman also looked for promising and popular properties in the most traditional medium of all — books — and negotiated for valuable licenses in the publishing arena.

Kate Pressman, Media Insider

There are many wonderful things about having a child in the household, especially if you run a toy and game company and even more especially when the child in question falls into the age group your toys and games are intended for.

You get to see firsthand and in real time what kids are attuned to in media-driven popular culture. You learn about what truly excites them — and soon discover that kids are a lot more discerning about their media than most parents think they are.

The leadership of Pressman was always attuned to what kids really wanted. As early as 1955, Lynn Pressman was open to inspiration from her children. Like many young children, they were afraid of going to the doctor, and this gave Lynn the idea that Pressman should develop doctor, nurse, and even dentist kits, all inspired by her intuition that such playthings would help her children — and all kids — cope with their anxieties. From a business standpoint, parents who were weary of dragging their children, kicking and screaming, to checkups would be motivated to give the kits a try. And they did!

Some forty years later, Lynn's son Jim turned to his daughter, Kate, for insight and inspiration. He paid close attention to what Kate was watching on TV at home. The result was a wealth of key licenses.

Thanks, Kate!

Cartoon Network debuted in 1992, and *Scooby-Doo!*, a Hanna-Barbera cartoon series that originally aired on the CBS TV broadcast network from 1969 to 1976, was revived as a Cartoon Network mainstay in 1993. It was an animated show featuring four teenagers – Fred, Daphne, Velma, and Shaggy – along with their talking Great Dane, Scooby-Doo, who solve supposedly (but not really) supernatural mysteries through a series of missteps.

Cartoon Network aired the original shows multiple times per week. Kate Pressman became a big fan in 1999, when she was four years old. Observing her devotion, Jim scented a licensing opportunity. After researching, he discovered that the show in fact aired some *twenty times* per week. This was indeed major exposure. But the really astounding

thing was that there were no *Scooby* toys or games under license!

Jim went to Warner Bros., the licensing agent, and made a deal. The time was ripe for it. Because no competitors had shown licensing interest, he was able to negotiate a very modest guarantee. As Jim already knew from experience, in licensing there was a big advantage in being a firstcomer. Of course, as he knew only too well, the risk was greater, too. But the potential reward made the venture worthwhile.

The 1999 Pressman catalog featured three *Scooby-Doo!* board games: the *Scooby-Doo! Get That Dog Game* (a card-matching game that sharpened youngsters' memory skills), the *Scooby-Doo! Mystery Mansion Game* (a board game in which players help Scooby catch the monster haunting the mansion),

Some of Pressman's extensive line of *Scooby-Doo!* products, which spanned from 1999 to 2014.

and the *Scooby-Doo! Thrills and Spills Game* (a more action-oriented board game involving yet another haunted house adventure).

All the 1999 games were branded with the Cartoon Network logo, and Scooby-Doo was already a well-known character. Nevertheless, potential retail buyers had to be persuaded, precisely because there were virtually no other *Scooby*-licensed toys on the market. So, as Pressman had done in the past – but never before with a licensed property – the new games were promoted by television commercials to increase confidence among retail buyers.

The *Scooby-Doo!* line also included puzzles, and *Scooby* proved instrumental in bringing puzzles into the Pressman line. In 1999, *Scooby* puzzles included the three-foot-tall *Scooby-Doo! Pal-Size Puzzle*, in addition to *Scooby-Doo! 24-Piece Puzzles* and *Scooby-Doo! 100-Piece Puzzles*.

As for *Scooby-Doo!*, it remained a part of the Pressman line until 2014 with a wide variety of games and puzzles. Most significant among these was the *Scooby-Doo! Pop 'n' Race Game*. First presented in 2008, it was not only a *Scooby* license but a licensed version of the popular game *Trouble*, which had been introduced by Kohner Brothers in the US back in 1965 and was subsequently a big seller for Milton Bradley (which later became a part of Hasbro). Over the years, a number of companies marketed licensed variations on *Trouble*, but the *Scooby-Doo! Pop 'n' Race Game*, a two-to-four-player racing game for ages five and up, was the first of these and one of the most successful.

Vienna Downes, Warner Bros. senior manager of toy licensing, recalled that "the Pressman *Scooby-Doo!* games were always one of the most fun product lines to develop. The product was innovative, clever, accessible, and fun for the entire family – a staple and cornerstone to the *Scooby-Doo!* merchandising program."

Thanks Again, Kate!

In 1988, Universal Pictures released to theaters *The Land Before Time*, an animated feature film produced and directed by Don Bluth and executive produced by George Lucas and Steven Spielberg. It introduced five young friends — four dinosaurs and a pterosaur — who find and raise a baby *Tyrannosaurus*, by the name of Chomper, and successfully pass through a number of adventures, learning life lessons and deepening their friendship in the process.

The feature launched a direct-to-video franchise, thirteen more movies, which, in the days before online video streaming, were released on DVDs. The video series began in 1994, and Kate Pressman became a fan around 2002. Her father duly took note, and Pressman introduced their line of *Land Before Time* games in 2003, by which point nine of the thirteen DVDs had dropped, almost one each year and always exquisitely timed for December release, which was perfectly coordinated with the peak holiday season for toy sales.

Clearly, *The Land Before Time* had a large fan base, but it was only thanks to the presence of Kate in the Pressman household that Jim was able to recognize that the fans were almost certainly ready for "product." Best of all, at this point, no "product" existed. Accordingly, negotiations were initiated, and another successful licensing venture was launched. Pressman produced both *Land Before Time* games and puzzles in 2003, including *The Land Before Time Great Valley Game* and a pair of fifty-piece puzzles, *Over the Falls* and *Taking a Swim*.

OPPOSITE
The *Scooby-Doo! Thrills and Spills Game* (1999).

ABOVE
The Land Before Time Great Valley Game (2003) was inspired by an animated film franchise from Universal Pictures.

Kate Pressman and her classmates visit the Pressman Toy factory in New Brunswick, New Jersey. Pressman continued to manufacture in the USA long after most other toy and game companies had moved manufacturing to China.

Getting Schooled

Young Kate Pressman had schooled her father on how to be the first to market with some of the best licenses of the new millennium. When she was five, Jim visited her kindergarten class, where he showed the kids different game concepts – to entertain them, of course, but, even more, to get a close-up idea of what they liked and what they didn't. The kids loved it, and Pressman Toy got the benefit of a spontaneous, ready-made focus group. Class teacher Ginny Katz has remained Jim's longtime Facebook friend.

About two years later, Jim gave his now seven-year-old daughter and her classmates an opportunity to visit Pressman's state-of-the-art toy factory in New Brunswick, New Jersey, to see toys and games in the making.

The school bus arrived in the morning at 745 Joyce Kilmer Avenue in New Brunswick, and the class met with Jim, who shared with them some of the current line. Then the factory tour began with a visit to the Injection Molding Department. The machines were creating game parts for everything from checkers to *Gooey Louie*, some operations performed by human operators, others by autonomous robotic arms.

The children saw the process from start to finish, led along the manufacturing lines to the end of the belt, where games were boxed and wrapped in shrink film. After the tour, they were treated to a McDonald's lunch. The first factory tour was in 2002, and Pressman repeated them in 2003 and 2004.

Jack Pressman Enters the Hall of Fame

In 1984, the Toy Industry Hall of Fame was established to recognize the people who had built the industry. Induction into the Hall is an honor bestowed upon two to three individuals annually, and in 2009, Jack Pressman was inducted.

Long overdue, it was a moving occasion. All the company's executives and key employees attended the TOTY Awards presentation at Chelsea Piers in Manhattan, where the latest additions to the Hall of Fame were honored. Jack's children, including Jim, of course, were there. At Jim's request, Hasbro's Alan Hassenfeld made the speech introducing Jack's induction.

For Lynn Pressman, now ninety-seven years old and failing in health, the occasion was the last time she ventured out of her home. In a poignant moment during the ceremony, Lynn stood and accepted the accolades from the crowd. Five months later, in July 2009, she passed away, having lived a remarkable life that enriched the lives of her children and so many others.

The last time the ninety-seven-year-old Lynn Pressman Raymond ventured away from her home was to attend the induction of her late husband into the Toy Industry Hall of Fame. Her passing, on July 22, 2009, merited a warmhearted obituary in *Playthings*.

G.S. SCHWARTZ & Co. Inc.

Public Relations

Obituary: Lynn Pressman Raymond

By Staff -- Playthings, 7/24/2009 9:12:00 AM

NEW YORK—Lynn Pressman Raymond, former president of Pressman Toy, passed away on July 22 at age 97.

Pressman Raymond served as president of the company for nearly 20 years, succeeding her husband, Jack Pressman, the founder of the company.

"At a time when few women entered the ranks of executives, Lynn ran the toy company in her own flamboyant and one-of-a-kind style. Known for her lavish parties, Mr. John hats, as well as her business acumen, no one ever came close to her style and panache," according to a company statement.

Born Lynn Rambach, Pressman Raymond married Jack Pressman in 1942, 20 years after he started his toy and game company. Within five years, Pressman had dissolved his business partnership with Max Eibetz and appointed Pressman Raymond vice president of the company.

While vice president, Pressman Raymond is credited with the idea for the company's popular Doctor Bag, a kit released in 1956 that was designed to help children overcome fear of doctors. The product was so popular it prompted Pressman to manufacture a Nurse Bag and, in 1962, Mattel-licensed Ken and Barbie doctor and nurse bags.

Following Jack Pressman's death in 1959, Pressman Raymond took over as company president, becoming one of only a handful of female executives in the toy business. Under her leadership, Pressman Toy became an early adopter of television as a means of promotion for games.

Pressman Raymond's son James (Jim) Pressman has run the company as president since 1979. Her other son, Ed Pressman, is a noted film producer.

Pressman Raymond attended the 2009 Toy Industry Hall of Fame induction ceremony to accept the award on behalf of her late husband.

470 Park Avenue South, 10th fl., New York, New York 10016 • Phone: (212) 725-4500 • Fax: (212) 725-9188
www.schwartz.com

Toy Industry Hall of Fame

Jack Pressman

1900–1959 · Inducted in 2009

Company: Pressman Toy Company

Greatest Hits: Dick Tracy, Little Orphan Annie, and Snow White toy lines; Chinese Checkers; doctor and nurse kits; Ping Pong sets

Jack Pressman

Jack Pressman grew up working in his father's variety store in Harlem selling school supplies, candy, sporting goods, and toys, which sparked his interest in the toy industry.

In 1922, Pressman founded J. Pressman & Co. with partner Max Eibitz. In the early years, Pressman's line consisted of all sorts of crafts, games, and activities. Everything from metal "Bolb Ball" (similar to Skillball), to wood "Child's Clothes Pins," a toy Zellaphone (like a xylophone), and much more.

As early as 1937, Pressman began seeing the value of licensing popular characters and matching them with new or existing products. Snow White crayon sets, Snow White cut out doll (1938), Little Orphan Annie bubble pipe (1937), and Quintuplets embroidery set (not licensed but based on a real life news story) are some early examples.

Their first hit was Chinese Checkers, which they acquired the rights to in 1928. Early sets were made of wood or metal, with glass marbles.

LEFT AND BOTTOM RIGHT
Jack Pressman's plaques at the Toy Industry Hall of Fame at the Strong National Museum of Play, Rochester, New York.

TOP RIGHT
Jack was inducted into the Hall in 2009, in a ceremony attended by the Pressman family: (*left to right*) Kate, Ed, Lynn, Jim, Ann, Ed's wife Annie, and Donna.

Playing Games in the New Millennium

For Pressman, the turn of the millennium teemed with games and puzzles, many of them the products of exciting new licenses, but not all!

A Game for Girls (2000)

Fib Finder resembled the popular parlor game *Truth or Dare*, except that here the arbiter of truth was a battery-operated "electronic" lie detector. One player would choose a provocative question from cards — "Do you have a crush on somebody?" — and ask another player. Usually, the answer would be evasive, but the Fib Finder would (somehow) detect the lie, emitting an electronic sound and a display of flashing lights. If the Fib Finder decided the answer was true, however, the player would advance on the game board.

The genius of *Fib Finder* was not in the game board or the flashing lights or even the game! It was in the magic and fun of conversation among a group of girlfriends. A TV commercial captured precisely this, not only explaining the game but making it a hit.

Fib Finder, from 2000, invited girls to tell the truth or fib. Either way, it was sharing.

For 2 to 4 players
Ages 7 and up

Pressman®

SPIDER-MAN

SPIDER-MAN vs the GREEN GOBLIN
Game

Collect all 5 SPIDER-MAN Powers and prepare
for the Final Battles against the Green Goblin!

OFFICIAL MOVIE MERCHANDISE

A Marvel license resulted in 2002's
Spider-Man vs. the Green Goblin Game,
among other Pressman offerings.

Marvel Becomes a New Marvel (2003)

Pressman had licensed Marvel superhero properties years earlier but returned to the Marvel Universe with a *Spider-Man* comic/movie license in 2003. A year earlier, Marvel had struck gold with the 2002 *Spider-Man* movie. It was just the first of what would prove a strong franchise of feature films — and one that is still going strong. In 2003, however, Marvel had yet to become a licensing juggernaut. For Jim Pressman, the indicator that it was high time for a new license came when his research revealed that Marvel comic books now far surpassed competitor DC in sales.

It seemed to be a tipping point, and Pressman once again was in the vanguard of what would become a Marvel licensing frenzy. With just a modest advance, the company secured the rights to both *Spider-Man* and *The Hulk*.

The first *Spider-Man* game blew off the shelves, and soon its success far surpassed Pressman projections for children of all ages. The company embarked on a whole series of *Spider-Man* and other Marvel-based games, including a trivia game, a *Marvel Heroes Chess Set*, the *Hulk Busts Loose* board game, and others.

Deal or No Deal and Howie! (2005)

Even with a tsunami of Marvel superheroes, there was no way Pressman was going to pass up new TV licenses. By the time NBC announced *Deal or No Deal* as a new primetime game show in 2005, Pressman had proved that it was *the* company that could make

TV game shows into successful home games. In this case it was the show's licensing agent who reached out to Jim, when Jim was visiting LA with his marketing VP.

Over the phone, Jim and the agent negotiated a deal for a $100,000 guarantee on a *Deal or No Deal* license. It was a very substantial figure, of course, but Jim knew he had to act fast because, in this case, Pressman was already bidding against competitors for the license. Clearly, the show had the makings of a winner. It put contestants in the position of choosing from a selection of briefcases, each of which contained a cash value of anywhere from a penny to a million bucks. As the game played out, the contestant eliminated cases and was from time to time offered a "deal" by the Banker to quit the game for a stated cash payment. The contestant could take the deal or refuse it. When only one case was left, the player had the choice of trading it for a case he or she had

chosen before play began. The prize was the money in the chosen briefcase. Could be a lot. Could be very, very little.

Brilliantly hosted by comic Howie Mandel, *Deal* was a very big deal for NBC and for Pressman. A year after the original board game came out, the company made a special version with a replica of one of the briefcases seen in the show and shipped it exclusively to Walmart.

While *Deal or No Deal* was a big hit for Pressman, it was nowhere near the magnitude of the earlier *Who Wants to Be a Millionaire?* Indeed, it proved to be the last time a primetime TV game show had a major impact on the toy industry. The kickoff for the game was spectacular, with Jim joining Howie Mandel in festivities at the Toys"R"Us flagship store in New York's Times Square. That was fun, but it was also the last hurrah for the blockbuster TV game shows – and licenses.

Deal or No Deal was a big-time hit for NBC TV – and for Pressman, too!

Hello Kitty (2007)

Hello Kitty was a licensing machine – but an adorable one – for Pressman and many others.

Target, a major Pressman customer, was the exclusive US mass retailer of the tremendously popular *Hello Kitty* line. The one category of *Hello Kitty* merchandise Target was missing – and very badly wanted – was puzzles.

They came to their game and toy partner, Press-man, and that meant they came to the right place. Pressman licensed *Hello Kitty* in 2007 and created a whole line of puzzles and games. Games included the *Hello Kitty Happy Seasons Game*, *Fortune Finder Game* (which came in an iconic *Hello Kitty* purse), *Flip 'n' Match Game*, and *Crazy 8's* card game.

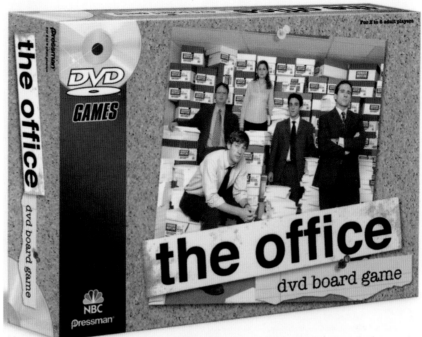

The Office—Never Underestimate the Power of a Fiercely Loyal Fan Base (2008)

Completely different were the Pressman board game and DVD game based on *The Office*. An American version of a UK original, *The Office* starred comic actor Steve Carell. It got off to a slow start when it debuted in midseason 2005 on NBC but by 2006 found its mojo. By the time Pressman secured a license and introduced its two games, *The Office* had a strong and extremely devoted fan base. One game was trivia-based, while the other included a DVD with

scenes from the TV show, which players watched and then answered questions relating to what they had just seen.

Like *Saved by the Bell* years earlier, the show was not a megahit, but those who loved it really loved it, were passionately loyal to it, and were motivated to buy spinoff products. For Pressman, the timing was just right, hitting the market at the peak of the show's popularity.

The American version of the quirky British TV sitcom *The Office* had a fanatically loyal following and was thus a natural for a Pressman trivia game and a DVD board game.

Pressman worked closely with Wimpy Kid author Jeff Kinney on the *Diary of a Wimpy Kid Cheese Touch* game in 2011.

Diary of a Wimpy Kid— Jeff Kinney's Hands-On Humor (2011)

The era of new media brought numerous predictions of the imminent demise of the traditional book. None of these prognostications proved true, and Jim Pressman identified the Wimpy Kid series of kids' books by Jeff Kinney as a licensing property worth a closer look. Fox had become the licensing agent because of its deal to make a movie based on *Diary of a Wimpy Kid*. Now, big companies like Warner Bros., Sony, and Fox can be hard-nosed negotiators, but they usually move the process ahead quickly because the decision-making authority is centralized. In the case of Wimpy Kid, however, Jeff Kinney was very hands-on. Deeply concerned about the quality of every detail licensed from his books, he insisted on creating new artwork for the Pressman games, including for the packaging. This unquestionably added to the quality of the product, but Jeff had so many projects on his desk that art and approvals were painfully slow in coming.

No matter. In the end, the result was worth all the time and nail-biting. Jeff's books, movies, and board games were all strong, steady sellers, and the *Diary of a Wimpy Kid Cheese Touch* board game, in which two to six players (ages eight and up) played their favorite characters in a race around the game board, proved to be the most successful game based on a book that Pressman ever had.

The Elf on the Shelf—Where's He Hiding Now?! (2013)

The Elf on the Shelf: A Christmas Tradition was a property that started out in 2005 as a kids' picture book, written in rhyme, which explained just how Santa Claus knows who's naughty or nice. (Turns out that he sends very small scout elves to live unobtrusively in homes and keep track of the family's children.) Eventually, the book was packaged with an elf doll, the idea being that the parent would hide the elf somewhere, so that he could carry out his mission of surveillance undetected.

The *Elf on the Shelf* doll phenomenon exploded on social media, on which hordes of parents posted the variety of strange places they hid the elves: in the refrigerator, under the toilet, atop a tower of toilet paper rolls, in the dryer, in a sock, in the car, in a jar, in a box of cereal, and between the sofa cushions—in fact, just about anywhere except on the shelf.

The internet turned *The Elf on the Shelf* into a sustained fad, and since the book already came with a toy, Pressman had to find ways to avoid interfering with the original. This resulted in *Where's the Elf on the Shelf?*, a matching game that exercises the memory and is suitable for ages three and up. Part of the challenge was creating packaging that persuaded the consumer that inside was a game, not the Elf character. Subsequently, however, another Pressman game, *The Elf on the Shelf Musical Game*, did feature an elf figure, but one that played music. Kids could follow the melody to the elf's hiding place.

The Elf on the Shelf, a 2005 kids' picture book packaged with a small elf, became *The Elf on the Shelf Musical Game*, a Pressman game from 2013.

Trash Pack — Never Too Gross to Win (2013)

In 2011, an Australian toy company, Moose Toys, developed a line called *Trash Pack*. These were small collectible figures that were packaged in a garbage can. For good reason. These "Trashies," as they were called, were basically gross, in a cartoonish sort of way — characters perfectly suited to living in a trash can. Like *Gooey Louie*, they were something boys really loved.

Pressman acquired a license and developed a line of games in 2013, including *Dash for the Trash*, among others. There were also puzzles, one of which was even cleverly packed in a *metal* garbage can. Jim had learned from his experience with *Gooey Louie* never to underestimate the power of the gross-out. The *Trash Pack* premise could not have been simpler, but Pressman's licensed products sold very well.

Shopkins — A Happy
Send-Off (2014)

Trash Pack was Pressman's last license before the company was sold to Goliath in 2014. In fact, perhaps the most significant result of the relationship that had been forged between Pressman and Moose Toys by the *Trash Pack* license was that it put Goliath, after it took over Pressman, in an ideal position to license Moose's next range of collectible figures.

Introduced in 2014, they were called *Shopkins*, tiny collectible toys — miniatures, really — each based on a grocery store item. While *Trash Pack* was a big hit, *Shopkins* was twice, maybe even three times, as big, giving Pressman's new parent company a home run right off the bat. The last chapter tells the story of how Pressman Toy joined the Goliath family.

Three Pressman catalog covers: 2001, 2002, and 2011.

Chapter 17
Goliath

2014–2022

By the beginning of 2014, Jim Pressman believed this could very well be the last year Pressman would remain under his family's ownership. Reflecting back on the forty-three years he had worked at the company and the thirty-seven of them during which he had been its president, Jim thought less in terms of toys, games, and money made and more about the accumulation of wonderful memories and so many dear friends, both allies and competitors. The 2014 Pressman catalog paid tribute to the past by placing the company's memorable 1954 logo front and center.

Owning a Company
Means Selling It—Someday

As far back as 1973, when Jim had first joined the company, there had been discussion about selling. The talk was renewed now and then over the years, as it is in most companies, especially those owned by families.

But the time never seemed right – because it wasn't.

Years went by until at last, in 2013, Jim Pressman began discussions in earnest to sell Pressman Toy Corporation. The prospective buyer was a North American corporation that is now a large publicly held company. It was time. Jim was turning sixty-five. Donna and Jim's daughter, Kate, was in college and had no interest in joining the company, let alone assuming its leadership. In short, Pressman Toy was on the verge of becoming a family company without a family. Besides, Jim and Donna looked forward to having more time to travel, something they both loved.

Deal or No Deal

The discussions with the potential buyer proceeded slowly, three steps forward, two back. They were also intended to be confidential, but whereas Jim kept the silence, the potential buyer did not. Word soon got out to the industry that Pressman was about to be sold. Such leaks can cripple a company because both employees and retailers begin to get nervous about working at a place about to change hands.

Adi Golad, a long-time friend of Jim's and the European licensee of Pressman's enduring hit *Tri-Ominos*, had started toy companies around the world and recently opened his own company in the USA, based in Dallas. He told Jim that he had heard Pressman was up for sale, and he wanted to talk about buying it. Having promised confidentiality to the potential buyer, Jim denied the "rumors." However, negotiations with the current suitor were not going in the right direction. Three steps forward, two back had become one step forward and two back. Besides, the prospect had already let the cat out of the bag.

When the period of confidentiality with the original potential buyer lapsed, Jim agreed to talk to Adi. More and more, selling to him seemed a great idea. The two men had a long-standing mutual trust and respect for one another, and they began to chat. Whereas the negotiations with the original prospect had always been awkward and painful, the more Adi and Jim talked, the more it seemed that the union of Goliath and Pressman had been predestined.

Gross Business

Gooey Louie – the hit game built on picking a stranger's nose – played a key role in the relationship. Back in 1996, Adi signed a deal with Jim to sell Pressman's unabashedly gross action game in Europe. It was an important step for Goliath because it was the first time the company had entered the action-game category. As such, acquiring *Gooey Louie* was high-octane fuel propelling the growth of Adi's company. European sales of *Gooey Louie*—and those of the many other action games that followed – eventually gave the organization the resources it needed to acquire Pressman. Jim and Adi agreed: *Gross is beautiful!*

Goliath's Adi Golad
with Donna Pressman
in Israel.

The Deal Is Done

There is no denying that selling a nearly century-old family company is an emotional proposition. It is all too easy for negotiations to get ugly and relationships to turn sour. But in this case, negotiations were overwhelmingly positive. They began during the Toy Fair in the small Airbnb apartment Adi Golad had rented near the Javits Center, where Toy Fair was held.

The discussions that unfolded there were quiet and pleasant, far less about an ending than a new beginning. They were two friends and colleagues talking about the future. The sale was announced on July 29, 2014, and Goliath simply picked up where Pressman had left off.

Thanks to the dedicated, hard-working employees of both Pressman and Goliath, continuity was seamless, with Jim staying on for a year as president of Pressman and then for another year in a consultative role.

The Pressman name and product line continued, and under the leadership of David Norman, president of Goliath's North American operation, the sales of Pressman games have steadily grown since the purchase.

We are pleased to announce that Pressman Toy Corporation and Goliath Games LLC have merged effective June xxx, 2014. Both Pressman's and Goliath's brands are well known in the marketplace and will continue to be managed and promoted separately. The Pressman brand has meant high quality toys since its launch in 1922. From winning the first ever Toy of The Year Game Award for Who Wants To Be A Millionaire to its success with Deal or No Deal, Scooby Doo, Wheel of Fortune and Hello Kitty and other licensed games, Pressman has been one of the most successful game developers over the last 90 years and its products have produced over one billion dollars at retail. Goliath is the new kid on the block. Since opening its doors in 1978, Goliath has grown to be one of the 30 largest toy companies in the world. In the USA, Goliath promoted more games on TV in the Spring of 2014 than all other toy and game companies combined.

Jim Pressman will continue as President of Pressman Toy Corporation and will oversee all sales, product development and licensing functions for the Pressman brand. David Norman will continue as President of Goliath Games, LLC. In addition to Mr. Norman's current responsibilities, he will also be in charge of developing TV advertising campaigns for Pressman's core brands and overseeing all back office functions for the combined companies which will be consolidated in the Plano, Texas office. The combined companies will be one of the top 3 game companies in the USA with a rapidly growing presence in other toy categories.

We are grateful to you for not only supporting our past growth but also for the opportunity to partner with you to deliver a collection of innovative, classic and great selling toys and games to consumers throughout the world. This is only the beginning.

_____
Jim Pressman
President, Pressman Toy Corp

_____
Adi Golad
Managing Director, Goliath
International Holdings

Draft of the press release announcing Pressman's sale to Goliath.

Shopkins

In 2015, Pressman (under Goliath's ownership) picked up the *Shopkins* license from the Australian company that had licensed *Trash Pack* to the company in 2013. The major reason they selected Pressman was their long-standing relationship with Jim Pressman.

   Trash Pack had been huge, but *Shopkins* was even bigger. Goliath proved highly skilled at maximizing sales, and sales of *Shopkins* games in 2015 and 2016 were greater than those of any other licensed games.

Amazon Rises, Toys"R"Us Falls

Toys"R"Us had been Pressman's largest customer for years. The company went private in 2005 when investors purchased it in a $6.6 billion deal with debt. But Toys"R"Us proved unable to consistently generate sufficient profit to pay back the debt and had no money to reinvest in store operations. Couple this with the rise of Amazon – which eclipsed Toys"R"Us in terms of selection, ease of shopping, and consumer pricing – and it is easy to understand why the once mighty brick-and-mortar chain just couldn't cut it any longer.

   Fortunately for Pressman and Goliath, the disappearance of Toys"R"Us did not bring an end to children's appetite for toys and games. Much of what had been Toys"R"Us sales quickly transferred to Amazon – and partly to other mass-market retailers. What changed is the way kids discover toys and games. Discovery very much shifted online, and toy marketing has never been the same.

These *Shopkins* products (2015) were a big hit for Pressman and its new owners.

A Game with No Losers

In 2014, Adi turned over day-to-day management of the global Goliath business to his son Jochanan. Under his leadership, Goliath has completed scores of additional acquisitions, and Goliath has grown to be one of the largest privately owned toy companies in the world. It even continued to expand its business during the Covid-19 pandemic as Goliath- and Pressman-branded products played a therapeutic role for many families, children, and adults living in anxious self-imposed quarantine.

In the coming months and years, Pressman will begin rereleasing many of its classic games from the past, as what is old seems to be what is new. In addition, it will expand how many of its long-standing titles can be played: not only on physical boards but also online and with apps. Product sales that were almost all in the USA a mere decade ago have now expanded and will continue to do so, making Pressman a truly global brand.

Pressman found a new home with a new family, and no one could have been happier. Jim Pressman is still on speed dial with his friends at Goliath/Pressman, as they continue to value his great advice. It is not often that both the buyer and the seller equally enjoy the outcome of a deal. This is the story of two great game companies. Perhaps it is only fitting that it ends as very few games do — with two winners.

Celebrating the sale and toasting the future at Jim and Donna's Manhattan apartment: (*left to right*) Jochanan Golad, Donna, Adi Golad, Jim, Kate, and Jael Golad. And Adi and Jim.

Toy Industry Hall of Fame

Jim Pressman

Inducted in 2022

Company: Pressman Toy Company

Greatest Hits: Rummikub, Matermind, Gooey Louie, Tri-ominos

Jim Pressman
Jim Pressman began his career at Pressman Toy Corporation in 1971, became president in 1979, and ran the company for 35 years, leading it with great success and integrity before selling it in 2014.

Under his direction, Pressman Toy was a pioneer of licensing and one of the first to promote board games via TV advertising. It was also among the first toy companies to bring TV game shows to market as board games, including Who Wants to be a Millionaire, Wheel of Fortune, Deal or No Deal, and Double Dare, creating a new genre of games and changing the way millions of Americans experienced game shows.

Pressman supplemented these licensed products with classics, becoming a leading supplier of chess, checkers, backgammon, and Chinese checkers (which the company introduced to the U.S. market). He also had an incredible eye for product and marketing, launching top hits such as Rummikub, Mastermind, Gooey Louie, Hydro Strike, Let's Go Fishin', Topple, and Tri-ominos.

Jim Pressman's plaques at the Toy Industry Hall of Fame at the Strong National Museum of Play, Rochester, New York.

Afterword
Jim Joins Jack in the Hall of Fame

On August 31, 2021, the Toy Association announced that the Toy Industry Hall of Fame was, "after a month of voting and consideration," inducting "two living legends" and two posthumous honorees into the Toy Industry Hall of Fame.

Robert Moog, founder of University Games and a Toy Association member, called Jim with the news: "Pinch yourself. You are really going into the Hall of Fame with Jack. I think only the third father/son combo after the Hassenfelds and the Sheas. Incredible." Bob and Jim had been close friends since Jim licensed University's big hit game, *Twenty Questions*, from him in 1987.

Another dear colleague and friend, Jill Hall, se-

nior manager of trends and partnerships at Tru Kids Brands, texted Jim that same day. She knew Jim from her days as the Toys"R"Us game buyer. "Hello Jim – I just wanted to send you sincerest congratulations on your Hall of Fame appointment – so absolutely well deserved! I think of you often and please know how very much I appreciated your friendship and support over the years – I am so very thrilled for you. All the best!"

It was none other than David Norman, president of Goliath Games North America, who was among those who had nominated Jim. At Goliath USA, David Norman continues to keep the Pressman name very much alive and well as it enters its second century in the American toy industry.

Jim was surprised by the news.

"I cannot believe it. My wonderful wife and best friend, Donna, and I have visited the Strong National Museum of Play multiple times in the past couple of years in order to do research for this very book that celebrates Pressman's centennial anniversary. Each time we visited, we took time to tour the Hall of Fame there. The names there are legendary, including my father, Jack, who, coincidentally, ran the toy company for thirty-seven years, the exact number of years that I was president. For me to be included with this group is a humbling experience."

Acknowledgments

We want to thank the following people for their contributions, without which this book never would have become a reality. Donna, Alan, and I truly appreciate all the resources that we were able to access in order to bring our dream of telling this story to life.

Robert Abrams
Kelly Adams
Charles Baum
Misha Beletsky
Penny Bernstein
Jamie Delson
Julie Doverspike
David Fabricant
Leslie Fine
Victoria Gray
Mary Higbe
Beth Merkle
David Norman
Julie Novakovic
Ira Resnick
Nicolas Ricketts
Jordan Rost
Hollis Stair
Harvey Stein

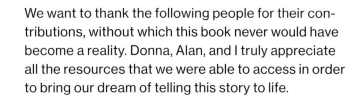

Index

Page numbers in *italics* refer to illustrations.

FRONT COVER: Pressman games throughout the years. Clockwise from bottom left, *Bingo* (see p. 23), *Rummikub* (see pp. 150–51), *Tiddledywinks* (see pp. 30–31), *Wheel of Fortune* (see pp. 160–62), *Let's Go Fishin'* (see pp. 174–75), and *Hop Ching Checkers* (see pp. 17–19).

BACK COVER: An assortment of Pressman's Basic Games, also known as the Red Line. (See pp. 147–49.)

PAGE 2: Three presidents of Pressman Toy with examples of their iconic products. From left, Jack Pressman with *Hop Ching (Chinese) Checkers* (see pp. 17–19), Lynn Pressman with *Doctor and Nurse Bags* (see pp. 68, 95), and Jim Pressman with *Wheel of Fortune* (see pp. 160–62).

PAGES 226, 232: Pieces from a Pressman Basic Games checkers set.

Editor: David Fabricant
Copy editor: Stephanie Baker
Production editor: Lauren Bucca
Designers: Misha Beletsky and Ilya Bernshteyn
Production manager: Louise Kurtz

First edition
10 9 8 7 6 5 4 3 2 1

ISBN 978-0-7892-1444-7

Library of Congress Cataloging-in-Publication Data available upon request

For bulk and premium sales and for text adoption procedures, write to Customer Service Manager, Abbeville Press, 655 Third Avenue, New York, NY 10017, or call 1-800-ARTBOOK.

Visit Abbeville Press online at www.abbeville.com.

Photography Credits

All photographs are courtesy of Pressman Toy or the Pressman family, with the exception of the following.

Gift of Charles Baum: p. 86

Copyright © 1965 the New York Times Co. All rights reserved. Used under license: p. 122 right

Collection of Ron Platt: p. 107 right

Documents researched by Jordan Rost: p. 9

Harvey Stein: p. 224 (photograph of Jim Pressman)

Courtesy of The Strong, Rochester, New York: pp. 2 (headshots), 10 top, 10 bottom right, 14, 15, 22 center, 22 top right, 22 bottom right, 33 center, 52 bottom, 53, 54, 60 bottom right, 62, 64 left, 72 left, 76, 78, 79, 80, 81, 88 left, 97, 100 top, 100 bottom left, 105, 107 left, 108, 109, 110 left, 124, 126 left, 132 right, 137, 144, 166 left, 196, 208 left, 208 bottom right, 224